Modern Greece

A Captivating Guide to the History of Greece, Starting from the Greek War of Independence Through the Balkan Wars, World War I and II, to the Present

Free Bonus from Captivating History (Available for a Limited time)

Hi History Lovers!

Now you have a chance to join our exclusive history list so you can get your first history ebook for free as well as discounts and a potential to get more history books for free! Simply visit the link below to join.

Captivatinghistory.com/ebook

Also, make sure to follow us on Facebook, Twitter and Youtube by searching for Captivating History.

Contents

Introduction

You may think you know Greece, but I'll wager that most of your knowledge ends at about the 2nd century BCE (Before Common Era) with the Roman conquest of the Greeks in 146 BCE.

You're not alone. For most people, including a lot of Greeks (especially in the Greek emigrant community worldwide, "the Greek diaspora"), Greek history is filled with stories of the gods, of Zeus, Apollo, Athena, Aphrodite, Poseidon, and many more. Then there are the heroes of Greek myth: Achilles, Ajax, Jason and his Argonauts—the list goes on. Then there are the thinkers: Socrates, Plato, Pythagoras, Hippocrates, Aristotle...and again, the list goes on and on.

Perhaps you are one of the relative few that are aware that in the early 19th century, British and other European writers, thinkers, and politicians fell in love with the idea of a renewed and glorious Greece based on the ideals of ancient times. You can see this idea in the following, which was written by George Gordon, better known as Lord Byron:

The Isles of Greece

The isles of Greece, the isles of Greece!

Where burning Sappho loved and sung,

Where grew the arts of war and peace,
Where Delos rose, and Phoebus
sprung!
Eternal summer gilds them yet,
But all, except their sun, is set...
The mountains look on Marathon—
And Marathon looks on the sea;
And musing there an hour alone,
I dreamed that Greece might still be free;
For standing on the Persians' grave,
I could not deem myself a slave.
A king sat on the rocky brow
Which looks o'er sea-born Salamis;
And ships, by thousands, lay below,
And men in nations--all were his!
He counted them at break of day—
And when the sun set, where were they?
And where are they? And where art thou?
My country? On thy voiceless shore
The heroic lay is tuneless now—
The heroic bosom beats no more!
And must thy lyre, so long divine,
Degenerate into hands like mine?
'Tis something, in the dearth of fame,
Though linked among a fettered race,
To feel at least a patriot's shame,
Even as I sing, suffuse my face;

For what is left the poet here?

For Greeks a blush--for Greece a tear...

Fill high the bowl with Samian wine!

Our virgins dance beneath the shade—

I see their glorious black eyes shine;

But gazing on each glowing maid,

My own the burning teardrop laves,

To think such breasts must suckle slaves.

Place me on Sunium's marbled steep,

Where nothing, save the waves and I,

May hear our mutual murmurs sweep;

There, swanlike, let me sing and die:

A land of slaves shall ne'er be mine—

Dash down yon cup of Samian wine!

Byron's obvious love of Greece led him to go there in the 1820s to help the Greeks in their war of independence against the Ottoman Turkish Empire. His death there rallied many other Europeans to the Greek cause, though it came by illness, not in battle.

Perhaps you know of Byron, but perhaps not.

Maybe you're a part of the early "Baby Boomer" generation and know a bit of Greece's story in WWII through the book and movie *The Guns of Navarone* (1961), a thoroughly fictional and barely informative "action" movie.

Then, of course, there's *Zorba the Greek* and its soundtrack. Millions of older British and Americans think they know a bit about Greece and Greek culture from this (admittedly outstanding) movie based on the even better book by Nikos Kazantzakis. *Zorba the Greek*, unfortunately, fed into many of the stereotypes Greeks face even today—great lovers of life who will dance for any reason, laugh in the face of tragedy, and drink, eat, and love their lives away.

My Big Fat Greek Wedding (2002), by Greek-American comic Nia Vardalos, told the story of an extended family of Greek immigrants in Chicago. They love to dance, eat, declaim on how everything good in the world, especially language, is a product of Greece and the Greeks. Oh, and the grandmother hates the Turks—can't forget that. The movie was hilarious, and while it includes some serious stereotyping, most Greek immigrants (or descendants of the same) will recognize the many truths held within. No mint jelly on the lamb—remember that.

And that's likely it. Perhaps you, too, are the descendant of Greek immigrants and want to know more about what Greece has done in the roughly two thousand years since the Golden Age of Greece. Or perhaps you're just curious about what happened to Greece. One day, it was at the top of the world, the apex of civilization, and the next?

Captivating History's *History of Modern Greece* is going to try to fill those gaps.

Chapter 1 – 1,453 years in a Short Chapter

One thousand four hundred and fifty-three seems like a really arbitrary number, but it is not. In the year 1453 CE, the Ottoman Turks finally seized the Byzantine Greek city of Constantinople (today's Istanbul). With the Turkish conquest of the city, what was left of Greece's former ancient glory was taken away, never to be returned.

Even during Rome's long rule over Greece, the Greeks supplied educators, writers, tutors to emperors and their families, musicians, architects, and doctors to the Romans. Much, although not all, of later Roman civilization had its roots in Greek antiquity, including its gods, which were mostly rebranded Latin versions of the Greek originals.

Even before the rise of Rome to world power, the people of the Italian Peninsula had had contact with Greece. Greece had colonies in southern Italy, Sicily, and along the Adriatic coast. Greek colonies even existed for a time in southern France.

To Julius Caesar and the Romans before and after him, Alexander the Great was *the* model of everything they wanted to be, and some Roman emperors would even claim they were descended from Alexander or were even Alexander reincarnated.

However, in history, glory is fleeting, and while the Romans' awesome military abilities allowed them to gain an empire far greater in size, strength, and duration than Alexander, they, too, were subject to the shifting sands of history. By 324 CE, the Roman Empire was in decline, battered by corruption and much else from within, as well as the "barbarian" attacks of the many different tribes of northern and central Europe.

By the late 5th century, Rome, as it had been known, had fallen prey to the many Gothic tribes that had assailed her for over a hundred years. However, the spirit of Rome and also of ancient Greece lived on in the Eastern Roman Empire, which began upon the declaration of Emperor Constantine ("the Great"), the first Christian Roman emperor, that the "new Rome" would be located at the crossroads of Europe and Asia in the new city of Constantinople, which the emperor dedicated on May 11th, 330.

The size of the Byzantine Empire (also known as the Eastern Roman Empire) waxed and waned for many years. It mostly waned, but at its height, under Justinian I (b. 482-d. 565; r. 527–565), it included parts of the old Roman Empire.

As you can see from the map above, the empire was assaulted by a variety of people for centuries, but it managed to survive until the mid-15th century, which was when the Ottomans finally captured Constantinople.

Various Turkish tribes had migrated westward from the steppes of central Asia, entering Asia Minor and the Caucasus areas in the early 7th century. Soon after their arrival, they were exposed to the spreading religion of Islam, which was carried by Arab tribes into the region after the death of Muhammad the Prophet in 632. From the 7th century to the 13th century, the armies of Byzantium (another name for the Byzantine Empire) and the Turks clashed with regularity, with one side temporarily gaining the advantage for a time only to lose it. In between wars, trade did go on with the Turks, who supplied raw materials and food items to the Byzantines (who, by this time, were almost exclusively ruled by emperors of Greco-Roman or pure Greek heritage) in exchange for gold and beautiful finished works of jewelry and much else that was, at that time, beyond their abilities.

In 1280, a powerful Turkish tribal leader named Osman united the various Turkic tribes of the area into a new entity—the Ottoman Empire, with "Ottoman" being an English term for "Osman." Osman is known to history as Osman I or, in Turkish, Osman Ghazi ("Osman the Conqueror"—sometimes the word "ghazi" referred to "raider" and sometimes "Conqueror of Christians" or "Infidels"). With the ascension of Osman and his uniting of the Turks under one banner, the war against the Byzantines became a war for not only power but also domination of the Turks (for they took over many Arab lands as well) and the religion of Islam.

By the beginning of the 13th century, the Byzantine Empire was a shadow of itself. It consisted of the still rich city of Constantinople. a small part of European Thrace, the Peloponnese (the southernmost part of Greece), and some islands. In 1453, the siege of Constantinople began.

The siege lasted for fifty-three days, from April 6th to May 29th. The Ottoman army numbered close to 200,000 men and perhaps 60 cannons. The Byzantines could only put together an army of about eight thousand, and most of those were foreign mercenaries. The emperor had sent out a call for men throughout Europe to defend his capital, which had been regarded by many as the successor to the glory of ancient Rome, but his call for help went unheeded.

The battle was won before it was over. Aside from their great numerical advantage, the Ottomans possessed the most and best of new technology. One of their largest guns weighed tons—four hundred men and sixty oxen had to pull it. The barrel of this "bombard" ("siege gun") was thirty inches in diameter and fired huge solid marble balls at the walls of the city. Initially, the guns caused panic more than anything else, but as more and more of the huge cannonballs struck Constantinople's walls, which were not in the best of shape to begin with, they began to collapse in huge chunks. Eventually, the Turks and their allies swept into the city, and over one thousand years of Byzantine history came to an end.

When Constantinople fell, much of Europe panicked, though many of its leaders had had the chance to aid the city. The city was not only the last political link to ancient Rome but also the center of Greek (or Eastern) Orthodoxy, one of the two dominant Christian belief systems of the time. From this time until relatively recently, the center of Orthodoxyshifted to Russia.

One of Byzantium's lasting contributions to Greece was its religious iconography (the painting of icons). While the rest of Europe was entering the Renaissance and experimenting with new techniques in painting (especially the use of perspective), the Byzantines continued to create beautiful, often gilt with gold, two-dimensional icons depicting scenes from the Bible, mostly the New Testament. This art form survives today in the nations dominated by the Orthodox Church (Greece, Russia, Serbia, and Bulgaria). Though icons exist in the Catholic Church, in the Orthodox Church, they take on greater meaning and import. Simply put, the idea is that the icon is not just a depiction of a holy scene but creates in the viewer some idea of holiness and is said to be a "window on the Divine."

Chapter 2 – Greece in the Ottoman Empire

It is impossible to tell the story of modern Greece, which essentially begins in 1821 with the Greek War of Independence, without discussing the Ottoman Empire. The Greeks and the Ottomans were intertwined for centuries, and one cannot understand the events of the 1820s without some background. The history of the Ottomans in Greece and the lives of the Greeks as part of the Ottoman Empire is rich and long—almost twice as long as American history.

From 1461, when the majority of Greece (mostly but not completely on the mainland) fell under Turkish rule, until the time of Napoleon Bonaparte in the late 1700s to early 1800s, Greece was controlled by two major powers: the Ottomans and the Venetians (the Italian city-state of Venice). The Italian city-state of Genoa also controlled a number of Greek islands for a time. (Interestingly enough, many of the residents of the Greek island of Chios, which figures large in the history of the War of Independence, believe that explorer Christopher Columbus was actually a Genoese born on Chios. We do know that he visited the island at some point.)

The Venetians and the Ottomans had a strange relationship. At times, they were on good or at least peaceful terms, trading with one another and angering more conservative elements within their respective empires and alliances who felt that war should be taking place between the "True Believers" and the "infidels" (substitute Muslims and Christians interchangeably).

For quite a long time, the Venetians had a distinct advantage at sea and used their economic and naval might to press the Ottomans into trade. On mainland Europe and, of course, in Asia Minor (and eventually the whole Middle East and the coast of North Africa), the Ottomans, with their immense and powerful armies, had the advantage.

Of course, at times, these two powers went to war with one another over the centuries. The unfortunate part, at least from the Greek point of view, is that not only were they powerless spectators in the conflict, but it was also their lands that were being fought over. Their cities were attacked, farmlands were destroyed, and the economy was ruined from time to time. "Luckily," this happened on a relatively local though large scale. However, on top of that, their women were subject to rape and kidnapping, and their men were subject to being put in chains as slaves. Both the Venetians and the Ottomans were perpetrators in this, with the Ottomans likely taking more Greeks as slaves to locations nearby.

Slaves were needed everywhere but perhaps most importantly for the navies of the respective powers. In 1571, the Ottomans fought a collection of Christian powers at sea in the Battle of Lepanto, which brought an end to the "Age of the Galley" and marked the beginning of the "Age of Sail." But until then, both sides needed men to power both their war and merchant ships. Galley slaves were chained to the benches. In most cases, when the ship went down, the slaves did too; they weren't worth saving and risking one's life for.

For the Venetians, the richest and most important islands were the Ionian Islands on the northwest side of Greece across from the Italian

Peninsula. They were not only close by and easier to defend but also provided an important staging area and transfer point for products coming from the area of modern Lebanon and Israel and, to a degree, spices from farther east in Persia and India.

On the map above, you can see the location of the Battle of Lepanto, which will be discussed in more detail later in the chapter, which is on the western side of Greece and marked "1571." This was a vital area, and it was fought over many times, as the Gulf of Corinth leads along the northern Peloponnese toward Athens and the Aegean Sea. The use of the Gulf of Corinth took much time off the travel from the west to the east of Greece and vice versa.

Today's tourist island of Corfu was, at the time, the most important strategic island in the Ionian Islands. The island was heavily fortified by the Venetians, and four fortresses/castles looked out over the north and the south to guard both the approach from the south, the Mediterranean and Aegean Seas, and from the mainland through the Gulf of Corinth.

On the western side of Greece lies the large island of Euboea, which is located immediately offshore north of Athens and is separated from the mainland by approximately 2,300 feet at its narrowest point. Needless to say, this island was fought over many times and was heavily fortified.

In the south, the largest of the Greek islands, Crete, along with another large island farther east, Cyprus (a source of tension between the Greeks and Turks even today), as well as varying numbers of smaller Aegean islands, were fought over for centuries, as they provided both staging points for trade with Asia and the Middle East but also food and other trade goods—and, of course, slaves.

The Ottomans had expanded into Europe decades before their conquest of Constantinople. Naturally, this alarmed the Christian states of Europe, and many large and bloody battles were fought from the late 1300s until the 1600s on the Continent. But from the 12th century until the late 13th century, the Europeans (especially those living and ruling on the coasts) did not have much to fear from the Ottomans at sea. The Turks had been a land power since their expansion from central Asia, and until the dawn of the 16th century, the Europeans expected their domination of the sea, especially the Mediterranean, would continue.

However, in the last decade of the 1400s, the Ottomans began constructing a fleet to compete with the Europeans, especially the Venetians. For decades, the only real competition to the Venetians at sea were the ships of the North African and Middle Eastern corsairs. Corsairs were privateers or pirates, and like most criminals, they preyed on the weak, slow, and isolated. When the Turks began to grow their navy, they slowly but increasingly began capturing Venetian and allied trading vessels and raiding the coasts of Venetian-controlled territories for slaves.

In 1499, a war between the Ottomans and the Venetians broke out at sea, and the Venetians suffered a string of humiliating defeats. One of the key Ottoman victories was the conquest of Lepanto (not to be confused with the later Battle of Lepanto), which allowed them to better control access to the interior of Greece and to move into the Adriatic Sea if they so wished. The Venetians did win a small victory and gained control of a couple of small islands, but that was nothing compared to the loss of Lepanto, which led to mainland Greece being entirely in Turkish hands by 1503.

In 1520, a new Ottoman sultan, Suleiman I (also known as "Suleiman the Magnificent" or "Suleiman the Lawgiver"), who is considered to be the greatest Ottoman ruler, came to power. Under Suleiman, the Ottomans pressed forward into central Europe, completing their conquest of the northern Balkans, after which they pushed into Hungary, arriving at the gates of Vienna in 1529.

Suleiman the Magnificent.

Luckily for Christian Europe and unluckily for Suleiman, bad weather, sickness, and supply problems, combined with the tenacious defenders (who were outnumbered about ten to one), caused the siege to fail. Despite another failed attack on Vienna in 1683, Suleiman's expansion into Europe was the highwater mark of the Ottoman Empire in Europe.

All of this shows that Greece, whose ancient history was considered by many to be the zenith of civilization, had become a very small piece of a very large and powerful empire. Suleiman was determined to not only advance Ottoman interests and control into southern and central Europe but also conquer all of the Greek islands as well. If large islands such as Crete and Cyprus were in enemy hands, the Turks' supply lines and coastlines would be at risk.

One of the other large islands of concern to Suleiman was Rhodes, which lies just off the coast of southwestern Asia Minor (today's Turkey). The island was the headquarters of the Knights of Saint John (also known as the Knights Hospitaller, the Knights of Malta, or the Knights of Rhodes), which was a devoutly (one might say fanatical) Christian order of knights that had been expelled from their home in the Holy Land in 1306 by Muslim forces. By the time Suleiman came to power, the Knights of Rhodes had become known less for their devoutness and more for their piracy, which cost the sultan large amounts of treasure. Despite the knights' Christian faith, they preyed on both Ottoman and Christian shipping.

Still, when the island fell to an immense and powerful Ottoman siege in 1521, the knights evacuated to Malta, where they would later fight the Turks in an epic siege in 1565. The Ottomans added more land and tens of thousands of more Greek subjects to their realm after the siege of 1521.

From 1521 to 1534, the Venetians and the Ottomans were at peace, but everyone knew it was only a matter of time before war began again. In 1540, the Venetians sued for peace, having lost almost all of their Greek territories to the Turks except for some tiny islands and the large and important island of Cyprus, which is just over 550 miles southeast of Athens in the Mediterranean.

From 1540 until 1570, the Venetians carried out trade with the Ottomans to the dismay of many Europeans, both the powerful and the poverty-stricken. However, in 1570, a new Ottoman sultan, the son of Suleiman, known to history as Selim II "the Sot" (a drunk, despite the Muslim stricture on alcohol), wanted to expand the empire even further and outdo his great father by winning a major victory at one of the oldest Venetian outposts in the Mediterranean and conquer Cyprus.

The Venetians, despite having angered many Europeans, including the pope, by trading extensively with the Ottomans, called upon them to help them save Cyprus when the Turks attacked in the late summer of 1571. The Papal Navy (yes, the pope had a navy) and the Spanish sailed to Cyprus, where they argued amongst themselves and left without engaging the Turks. Without aid, Nicosia, the capital city, fell in September, and the rampaging Ottoman soldiers killed thirty thousand people and took many more into slavery.

The last outpost of Venice on Cyprus was the fortress of Famagusta. The powerful fortress held out throughout the summer, fall, and winter of 1570/71. In the spring, Selim brought 200 ships and 250,000 men to Famagusta. The city held out against a powerful siege, in which over 150,000 cannonballs, some of which were huge, were fired at the fort, but on August 1st, the Venetians and their mercenary allies could hold out no longer. What happened next enraged Christian Europe and marked the beginning of a slow decline of the Ottoman Empire on the Continent and in Greece.

The commander of the Christian forces in Famagusta was Venetian Marcantonio Bragadin (sometimes spelled Bragadino). Bragadin accepted the Ottoman terms of surrender but likely did not envisage his own fate. By the time Bragadin surrendered, the Turks had lost thousands of men in the Cyprus campaign, as well as much treasure, so they decided to use Bragadin as an example to people as to what might happen should they oppose the Ottomans.

First, Bragadin was forced to endure a mock execution (head on the chopping block, etc.). Then, his nose and ears were cut off. After that, he was forced to crawl about the fortress on his hands and knees, kissing the ground. And as if that were not enough, he was tied to a chair and hauled to the top of a galley mast, where he was flayed (skinned) alive. His skin was then stuffed with straw and paraded through the streets, and what remained of him was then cast into a jail cell.

Before Famagusta, it might have been possible for the Venetians and the rest of Europe to make peace with the Turks or at least engage in trade agreements. But once word of Bragadin's fate spread through Western Christendom, a fire was ignited under the Europeans.

Occasionally throughout history, a battle will occur that changes history in an instant and forever. One of those was the Battle of Lepanto on October 7th, 1571.

Illustration 1: The Battle of Lepanto, attributed to the Italian master Tintoretto.

https://commons.wikimedia.org/wiki/File:Battaglia_di_Lepanto.jpg

At Lepanto, the Europeans of Venice, Spain, Genoa, Savoy, Tuscany, the Papal States, the Knights of Malta, and the Italian city-state of Urbino, as well as some English and French and a number of Christian adventurers, arrived with over 206 galleys, 6 galleasses (smaller but sometimes more heavily armed galleys), and 60,000 men (40,000 sailors and 20,000 soldiers). The Ottomans had 222 galleys with about 60 small galliots, which altogether carried 13,000 sailors, 35,000 men, and nearly 40,000 galley slaves (oarsmen).

In a battle that lasted all day and involved the massive exchange of cannon and musket fire at close range, as well as bloody boarding parties in which no quarter was given or taken, the European navy prevailed, having inflicted much more damage on the Turks than they themselves had sustained. Ironically, some of the commanders and soldiers of the Turkish fleet were Greek, as the Greeks had made their living off the sea since time immemorial. Many of the slaves in the holds of the galleys were Greek; this disparity in treatment will be explained in the next chapter.

The victory at Lepanto was celebrated throughout Europe, and it marked both the end of the "Age of the Galley" and the beginning of the "Age of Sail," as well as the highwater mark (so to speak) of the Turkish expansion in Europe. The last great Turkish conquest over Venice took place when the Ottomans conquered Crete in 1669 after a campaign that took fifteen years.

The Greeks had seen their islands and seas used as a battlefield between the Venetians and other Europeans and the Turks for over two hundred years. From the end of the Battle for Crete in 1669 and the start of the Greek War of Independence in 1821, the Greeks suffered, endured, and sometimes even thrived under Ottoman rule.

Chapter 3 – Greece and the Greeks under the Ottoman Rule

Even today (June 2021), feelings can run quite hot between the Greeks and Turks (the inheritors of the Ottoman Empire, which, though run from Constantinople and founded by the Turks, consists of many nationalities).

The latest tensions are due to the ongoing refugee crisis, with people mainly fleeing from war-torn Syria. As of this writing, the Turks are urging Syrian refugees who have fled to Turkey to continue on to other European nations, which is the goal of most refugees. However, since the avalanche of Syrian refugees in 2015, many of the other European countries have been less than eager to take in more of them. Under an agreement made in Brussels with European Union members in 2016, Turkey had agreed to hold Syrian refugees while they were vetted for admission into Europe. All the countries involved have become overwhelmed by the problem, and in the last year, Turkey has pushed (sometimes literally) refugees over its border with Greece, which has attempted to house refugees in camps among its various islands near the Turkish coast.

Tensions have run so high that tear gas has been shot toward either side, either at one another's troops while refugees are pushed forward or sent back or at the refugees themselves. Naturally, each side blames the other for the problems that exist along their border.

Before the Turks even arrived in Asia Minor, the Greeks and the residents of what is now Turkey were fighting. Geography has played a major role in the hostilities, but so have religion and culture. Then, of course, add in grievance after grievance stemming from those wars and occupations, and you have a recipe for disaster.

However, while many people in Greece and Turkey know of the problems and hatreds of the past, few realize that there have, at times, been cordial relations between the Turks and Greeks. Or rather between some Turks and Greeks, and those were mostly at the top of the socioeconomic scale, with some exceptions.

Like many an empire before and since, the Ottoman Empire depended on a few things in order to survive in the way to which it had become accustomed. For the first two and a half centuries or so of Ottoman rule in Greece, the Ottomans were at war, expanding their empire, or at least attempting to. Through the first part of Ottoman history, the empire and its sultan depended on wars for riches, power, and personal and imperial prestige. Without military conquests, the sultan was not able to reward his followers and demand their loyalty. And like so many other empires before, the Ottomans were subject to the same court intrigue, power struggles, and assassinations that came with leaders that were or seemed to be weak.

Greece was the most important Ottoman possession. From a prestige standpoint, the Turks were able to tell themselves and the world, "We have conquered the people who once ruled the world." Never mind that that was over one thousand years ago, but such was the power of ancient Greece in the popular imagination.

By the 1500s, the Ottoman Empire had become so large that it required more soldiers than were available in the Turkish population alone. Within a very short period of time, the Ottomans were taking in, either by way of volunteers or force, soldiers from other peoples. First, they took in Arabs and other people who had been Muslims since the Age of Muhammad nearly one thousand years before: Arabs, Egyptians, North Africans, Lebanese, Syrians, etc. However, as time went by and larger and larger armies and navies were needed, the Ottomans cast a wider net.

Greeks and other non-Muslim subjects could not serve in the army, except for one important exception. Greeks could become officers, especially in the navy. With increasing regularity and the bending of rules during the later Ottoman period, Greeks also became powerful figures at court and in the empire's administration, and they could often make or break other powerful figures, including the sultan himself.

The Ottomans were (in)famous for raiding the towns and cities of non-Muslims and taking their children to raise as Muslims and soldiers. These were the famous Janissaries (meaning "new army" in Turkish), whose ranks were filled with Serbs, Bosnians, Croats, Bulgarians, and other subject peoples, but they were mostly Greeks.

The Janissaries were fanatically loyal to the sultan, at least at the beginning of their history (they began in the 1300s and were banned in 1826 just after the Greek War of Independence), as long as the sultan was strong and provided them with opportunities for conquest, riches, and power. The Janissaries, the occasional powerful woman, who was usually but not limited to one of the sultan's wives or concubines, the court eunuchs, and others could sometimes play the role of kingmaker or, in this case, "sultan-maker."

The odd thing, as you can see, is that the Janissaries were frequently ordered to war on their own people. Since they had been taken as children and essentially brainwashed, it did not affect the Janissaries themselves to any great degree until later in Ottoman history, but it caused great resentment among the conquered for obvious reasons.

Even though a large part of the Greek population lived in the country's interior and was usually involved in some type of farming, a great many Greeks, then as now, lived near the coasts and have so for centuries. The Greeks, more than any other people in the Ottoman Empire by far, knew the sea. Greeks were some of the highest-ranking officers in the Ottoman navies, and they designed most of their ships and fleets and also captained and ran many of the Turks' merchant ships.

For those Greeks in the Janissaries, the Turkish navy, and the Turkish administration, life could be bearable or even good—sometimes very good. But for the vast majority of Greeks, living under Ottoman rule was sometimes a heavy burden.

The Turks considered their non-Muslim subjects not as people but as rayah, which means "cattle." These "cattle" were made to serve the Turks, mostly under a heavy tax burden. Intermittent and random raids would take slaves away from Greek villages, never to be seen again. As non-Muslims, taxes were high, and non-payment of taxes could bring severe punishment.

However, the Ottomans did not forcibly attempt to convert their subject peoples. As long as the Greeks and others fulfilled their duties to the sultan and obeyed the law, they were generally left in peace. Of course, there were numbers of Europeans who converted to Islam, most notably many of the Slavs of today's Bosnia. This was sometimes done out of genuine religious zeal but also to get ahead. Anyone who had converted could never return to the Christian faith, or they would suffer exceedingly unpleasant treatment under apostasy laws.

The overwhelming majority of Greeks belonged to the Greek Orthodox Church (just as they do today), though there was a significant minority of Jewish people, especially in the north in or near the city of Salonika. To the Turks, these were "People of the Book." Although they were not Muslims, they believed in the same God; they just did not acknowledge the Prophet Muhammad and his teachings. The Bible itself, along with the Jewish Torah and Talmud, were considered to be the revealed words of God through the prophets until the latest word, that of the Holy Quran.

As far as the established Greek Orthodox Church went, the Ottomans left it mainly alone. They knew the level of devotion the Greeks had for their church and realized that the institution could be useful in governing and maintaining control over the Greeks. In 1454, Mehmet the Conqueror confirmed the appointment of the Greek Patriarch Gennadios. From that point until the War of Independence (in which the church played a large part), the Greek Orthodox Church was considered an administrative branch of the Ottoman government.

The Ottomans did not impose Sharia law on their subjects but expected the Greek Church to keep order under their own written and unwritten rules. Though the Ottoman Empire was divided into administrative regions run by a governor or *hodijibashi*, most Greeks dealt with other Greeks when it came to government affairs.

During the time when Greece and the Greek isles were fought over by the Turks and the Venetians, many Greeks preferred to live under Turkish rule than Venetian rule. Part of this was historic. In 1204, the Venetians led a huge expedition of Europeans, ostensibly to the Middle Eastern Holy Land. But along the way, their giant fleet, carrying eighty thousand hungry and greedy western European warriors, stopped at Constantinople. Rather than go onto the Holy Land after being resupplied, they sacked the great Greek city. In Greece and much of the Mediterranean, memories stay for a long time. A very, very long time.

Adding to that, the Venetians treated the Greeks contemptuously, and to the Greeks, it seemed as if they were also attempting to establish the Catholic Church. The Venetians also placed a greater tax burden on them than the Turks, and while the Ottoman administration could be horribly corrupt, the Venetians apparently put them to shame. Very few Greeks were in the Venetian armed forces, either on land or sea, but quite the opposite was true regarding the Ottoman armies and navies.

Still, though many Greeks preferred the rule of the Turks over the Venetians, it was not as if Turkish rule was easy or celebrated by most Greeks; though as time went on, certain Greeks and Greek islands did benefit economically from their proximity to Turkey. Money aside, however, the Turks certainly let the Greeks know exactly what their status within the empire was, especially in the early part of the Turkish occupation.

The status of Greeks vis-à-vis their Turkish masters and their behavior was written in a series of codes and regulations. For instance, the Greeks were not allowed to bear arms or ride horses (though this usually meant dismounting at the approach of a Turkish official). Occasionally, a rule was enforced that forced Greeks to wear black clothing as a means of identification, as they could not wear Turkish-style clothes. Greek churches could not be built near mosques, and the common Greek (and Christian) practice of bell-ringing from church towers was tightly regulated as not to interfere with Muslim worship or holidays. The houses of Greeks could not be built taller or overlook Turkish homes or buildings nearby.

All of this was irksome but somewhat tolerable, and by the beginning of the 1800s, most of these regulations were honored in the breach and rarely enforced. What really bothered many Greeks was the imposition of heavy taxes, and Greece, especially those towns and cities near the coast, was one of the richest areas in the Turkish world. On top of that, as time went on, Turkish officials, as well as some Greeks, became more and more corrupt and constantly had their hands out for bribes.

However, the most resented aspect of Turkish rule was the devshirme or the "tax of children." This "tax" was enforced stringently at the beginning of the Turkish rule but fell off toward the end. However, the memory of it lingered on even after the Greeks had won their independence. The devshirme meant that Ottoman officials, not just in Greece but throughout the Christian parts of their empire, would tour the areas under their jurisdiction and select who they deemed to be the "most promising" Christian children for training in war and administration or both. These children would then be converted to Islam.

The strongest or most physically gifted among the boys would be sent to the Janissaries. These troops would be the sultan's and other officials' guards throughout the empire, as well as shock troops in battle. In a horribly ironic twist of fate, it was the Janissaries who were most often loosed on the subject populations when a point of discipline had to be made or a rebellion put down. In other words, these young Greek men, who had essentially been brainwashed into fanatical Muslim "holy warriors," would be turned upon their kinsmen.

Young men and boys gifted with intelligence would be trained as administrators and clerks to make sure the wheels of the empire kept turning. As in many warrior cultures, these jobs were "beneath" the Turks, and so they were filled by foreigners. A great many of them were Greek, not only in Greece itself but also in Asia Minor, other parts of the empire, and especially in Constantinople, where many Greeks rose to become quite influential figures by guiding policy, controlling budgets, gaining access to the sultan, and more.

As Muslim culture proscribed the painting or imagery of holy figures and greatly discouraged the image of sultans and other powerful figures, one of the Ottoman Empire's greatest contributions in the field of decorative arts was architecture. The greatest Ottoman architect was not Turkish, however, but Greek. His name was Sinan, and he was taken to Turkey in the devshirme in 1491. When he died in 1588, he was ninety-one and had created two of the most remarkable structures in the Ottoman Empire: the Suleimaniye Mosque in Constantinople and the Selimiye Mosque at Edirne in European Turkey or Eastern Thrace. Even today, eighty-four of his buildings can be seen just in Istanbul alone.

In addition to being important administrators and bureaucrats, the Turkish navy was filled with Greeks, not only as galley-slaves during the age before modern sailing vessels but also as captains, admirals, engineers/ship designers, and shipbuilders. When the Greek War of Independence began, the Turkish navy was at a serious disadvantage in both numbers of vessels and leadership.

During the very early part of the occupation, Turkish soldiers and sailors would raid the Greek coastline and islands for galley slaves. During the period just before the Battle of Lepanto (1571), tens of thousands of slaves were taken to power the sultan's ships. Galley slaves were not the only people forced into a life of slavery. Throughout the Ottoman Empire's history, it was powered to a great degree by slaves, who worked in the mines, fields, and homes of local and imperial officials. Naturally, this was resented by all of the subject people, not just the Greeks.

Of course, one of the most well-known aspects of Turkish rule was that of the harem. The word "harem" has many meanings. It can mean the section of a house (or palace) that is set aside for the women of the household. It can also refer to the women who lived there: wives, concubines, female relatives, and servants. Lastly, and most infamously, it can refer to a group of women kept as the sexual partners of the same man, who was almost always someone who held some power and wealth. (Some of these women were real "partners," married or not, and they often played the role of adviser.) Of course, many of the women and girls of the harem in this last sense were not there by choice. Like they did with the strongest and smartest boys, Ottoman officials and raiding parties would frequently take the most beautiful girls and/or young women to serve as sexual slaves for some powerful official.

In rare cases, concubines in the harem of the sultan or other high officials might wield some influence, as in the case of a Slavic girl from the area of southern Poland/western Ukraine named Roxelana, who is better known in Turkish history as Hurrem Sultan. She rose from being Suleiman I's (r. 1520-1566) favorite concubine into a woman of great influence at the sultan's court. In the middle of the 1600s, a number of these women managed to gain influence within the sultan's court, most famously a Greek girl from the island of Corfu named Kösem. Unlike Roxelana (who bore Suleiman a son who became the sultan himself, Selim II), Kösem and the other powerful women of the 1600s were ultimately put to death by the Ottomans' favorite method of execution—strangulation by bowstring. Of course, most of the kidnapped girls enjoyed no such fate and were destined for a life of sexual slavery and perhaps lived out their old age as a maid, nanny, or cleaning woman.

As you just read and as you likely know already, under a regime such as that of the Ottomans, it was dangerous, especially as a foreigner, to rise too high, too openly, too fast, or all three. One Greek, known to history as Ibrahim, rose from being a slave to a rich man in Istanbul, ultimately becoming the grand vizier (adviser to the sultan and the chief administrator of the empire). Unfortunately for Ibrahim, he made enemies in high places, which included the sultan's first wife. In the end, he was strangled by a bowstring. Another Greek, Michael Cantacuzenos, became one of the wealthiest and most influential merchants in Istanbul. In 1578, he, too, was strangled. His offense? Being an "over-mighty subject."

As horrible and as onerous as some of the treatment and laws of the Turks might have been, many Greeks lived their lives relatively untouched by them. In mainland Greece, especially away from the coasts, life went on much as it had before. In the cities of coastal Asia Minor and Eastern Thrace (now European Turkey), where the vast majority of people were Greek, not Turkish, the footprint of the Ottomans was relatively light. The Turks needed the economic benefits of these areas and peace in places so near the capital and heart of the empire. In Salonika, a great port and trading city whose population was mostly Jewish, religious rules kept the population in their place, but for the most part, as long as they paid their taxes and necessary bribes, the people of the city were left alone. Salonika was too important and too rich to interfere with on any great scale.

Throughout much of Greece, on the mainland and in the interior of the larger islands, small-holding farms were the economic order of the day. Again, as long as they paid their taxes, didn't complain too much, or rebel, the Ottomans let things be. In the often-mountainous and rugged Greek interior, ordinary Greeks oftentimes had more to fear from other Greeks than the Turks or their minions.

Bands of klephts, which can mean "thief" but is best defined by the word "brigand," roamed the countryside, especially in the remote mountainous areas. Many times, the klephts were organized around families and clans and were similar in many ways to tribal cultures in other parts of the world. Klephtic bands often plundered farms and villages of other clans, so a cycle of vendetta began. During and after the Greek War of Independence, the klephts were romanticized as heroic guerrilla warriors, and they were often just that. However, they often sold their services to the highest bidder and might later turn on them if a higher price was offered. During the War of Independence, bands of klephts were sometimes as feared as Turkish troops, as they would often march into a village, take away or kill the men, rape women, and steal whatever they could carry. Many Europeans and metropolitan Greeks, who had an idealized version of both the Greeks as a people and the klephts in particular, were disillusioned when bands of klephts carried out atrocities on Turkish or other ethnic groups during the war.

Klepht, circa 1820. Courtesy Getty Images.

Facing the klephts were bands of Greek and Albanian irregulars known as the armatoli. (Many Albanians lived in what is today northwestern Greece.) The almost constant warfare in the mountains and hinterlands of Greece caused an exodus to the coastal cities, such as Thrace and Constantinople, the latter of which may have been the most cosmopolitan of cities from the 1600s until the early 20th century.

By the late 1600s, the Ottoman Empire had started its long slow decline. One of the reasons for this was the rise in power of the western European nations and Russia, which limited Ottoman expansion. For a culture that counted itself among the great "warrior cultures" of the world, the end of expansion meant the end of plunder, and the end of plunder meant both heavier taxation on subject people and many dissatisfied soldiers.

Another problem was that an established system of succession had never existed among the Ottoman Turks. In many cases, by the late 1500s and early 1600s, a sultan came to power through court intrigue, military coup (usually and ironically carried out by the Janissaries, who were foreigners), assassination, or all three. Sultan Murad III killed nineteen of his brothers and seven pregnant royal widows to gain the throne.

This act of assassination was replaced by another equally destabilizing practice, that of "the cage." On the death of the sultan, his recognized heir would be almost literally "caged." He would be limited to the harem and not allowed access to the outside world. This might keep him safe, but it would also keep him ignorant of the world and his empire and what made it function. Many times, the empire was run by the chief eunuch, who was usually a sub-Saharan African, the sultan's chief wife, the grand vizier, who, as we have seen, could sometimes be a foreigner, or the Janissaries.

Mentioned above was the increase in taxation among the subject peoples of the empire. But this alone, while resented to a great degree, was perhaps not enough to push people into rebellion. High taxation rates can many times be overlooked if that money went to pay for the common welfare (land improvement, infrastructure, libraries, public safety, etc.). But by the end of the 1700s and early 1800s, these high taxes simply went into the pockets of the sultan, his court, or his administrators without making life better for the people. And since local officials seldom had enough money to carry out public works, things frequently only got done through bribery or influence. Not only did that mean that not much was improved, what was improved was the lives of those who could afford bribes. In other words, the rich got richer, but even the rich began to resent the high taxes that did nothing to better society.

One of the things taxes are supposed to pay for is public safety. Not only can violence lead to more violence and resentment, but economic progress also begins to grind to a halt. Throughout the empire, particularly in Greece, this is what began to happen.

In 1789, the French Revolution began. Like in other parts of Europe, the news of the progress, troubles, and terror of the French Revolution was followed in Greece. Among the many reasons for the revolution in France were the arbitrary and heavy tax burden and the corruption of the state and its officials.

While the devshirme was naturally resented, and very few people wanted to be ruled by outsiders, it's important to remember that for most Greeks under Turkish rule, life was not that different from people in the rest of Europe. Everywhere—in France, the states of Germany, and especially in eastern Europe and Russia—the lives of most people, who were often poor peasants, were hard. In eastern Europe and Russia, peasants had very few if any rights, including the right to choose what to do with their lives, where they could live, and much more. Even in western Europe, torture was commonplace for heresy and breaking the law, which could include criticism of the government or ruler, even into the 1800s.

People will put up with much if they are secure, but as the Ottoman Empire declined, the security of the people, especially in the countryside, became more and more tenuous. As the number of Ottoman conquests declined, the plunder available to the Janissaries did too. Throughout the empire but particularly in Greece, these elite troops began to prey on their own people. At times, the government representatives became worse raiders than the klephts in the mountains and hinterlands.

Of course, another factor in the rise of Greek resentment was religion. Again, while the population was able to worship relatively freely, and the church hierarchy worked with the Turkish government to keep order, Greeks, at the time and even today, were quite devout and resented not only the rule of the Turks but also their religion. In many cases, Greeks looked to the most powerful Orthodox power, the Empire of Russia, to help or even liberate them from Turkish rule.

In some cases, the tsars and tsarinas of Russia (meaning Catherine the Great, r. 1762-1796) paid lip service to the idea of helping their "little Orthodox brother" Greece, but for the most part, the Russians used this idea and threat as a bargaining chip against the Turks, with whom they frequently went to war.

However, in one case in 1770, Catherine sent two noblemen, the Orlov brothers, to Greece to foment rebellion while Russian troops fought the Turks for control of Crimea, a part of Moldavia, and other smaller territories around the Caspian Sea and Ukraine. Though the Orlov brothers did win one important naval victory, the expedition was a disaster, and they were forced to retreat back to Russia in the winter/spring of 1771. During the Russian expedition, the klephts of the Greek mountains organized, which was a feat in itself due to their constant infighting, and rebelled against the Turks in mainland Greece. In response, the Turkish government ordered hordes of Albanian guerrillas and Janissaries down into the Peloponnese, where they carried out brutal reprisals and atrocities.

The treaty that ended the war between Russia and Turkey (the Treaty of Kuchuk-Kainarji) gave the Russians an ill-defined right to interfere on behalf of Orthodox Christians in the Ottoman Empire and allowed Greek merchant vessels to fly the Russian flag for their protection. This allowed the Greek merchant fleet to grow into one of the largest in the world, but the Russians' "right" to interfere wasn't worth the paper it was written on, as they weren't going to go to war with Turkey over religious issues in Crete (for example). However, these provisions did give the Greeks hope that if they did decide to rebel, the Russians would be there for them. However, they were not.

Over the course of the French Revolutionary period and the rule of Napoleon afterward, Greek nationalism grew. This was partly due to the spread of the French Revolution's ideals and the Greeks' exposure to them in foreign ports. However, under the rule of Napoleon, what was left of the Venetian empire in Greece, as well as the Ionian Islands on the northwest coast, were occupied by France (1797). For a short time, France gave them over to Russia, doing so in 1799, but they were taken back by the French in 1807 under an agreement. During French rule, the French worked with an Albanian official of the Turkish government, Ali of Janina, who had amassed great wealth and a private army and was believed to have imperial aspirations in the Balkans.

All of this came to naught after the defeat of Napoleon. Some Greeks, mostly those living in Europe and among Greek intellectuals in the Ottoman Empire, believed that the Congress of Vienna (the gathering of nations brought together to discuss the maintenance of peace after years of war) would insist that the Turks give Greece at the very least some measure of autonomy, but this was wishful thinking. No one at the Congress of Vienna wanted to upset the status quo. Turkey had not been involved in the wars against Napoleon, except for when he had attacked Egypt, and the dominant statesman of the time, Austrian Count Metternich, along with Tsar Alexander I of Russia, did not want to encourage any more national revolutions.

Despite this, the French Revolution and the spread of representative governments in the rest of Europe had lit a fire under many Greeks. They saw the Ottoman Empire weakening from both within and without, and they began to make plans for the time when action toward independence seemed right.

The Road to Independence

By the start of the 18th century, Greeks within the Ottoman Empire and in the rest of Europe began to feel more "Greek" and less a part of the Ottoman Empire. This was helped by the ideas of the French Revolution but also by the beginning of the Romantic movement in

Europe, which, among other things, called for freedom of thought and expression for all men. Romantics yearned for a time in the past when freedom was the "rule of the day." They found this "Golden Age of Freedom" in the history of ancient Greece, particularly that of Athens.

Within Greece, the church began to teach young Greeks about their heritage, and wealthy Greek merchants in Greece, Asia Minor, and the rest of Europe began to establish libraries filled with books about Greece's "heroic" past that were written in Greek. Though this had not been forbidden under the Turks, it was certainly not encouraged, and throughout the time before the Renaissance, Greeks, like many other Europeans, were more concerned with survival than history. This was the situation for many in Greece after the Renaissance and until the time of the French Revolution. It is likely that the average upper- or middle-class Englishman in 1780 knew more about ancient Greece than many Greeks of the same social background.

The Greeks of the diaspora (those Greek living outside of Greece) were key in this revival of Greek identity and national feeling. Large Greek communities, centered around the many ports of Europe and even in Asia, as far as India, had gathered together, and for their own emotional and sometimes physical security, they lived together and valued their history as a way to retain their identity. The largest Greek communities of the time outside the Ottoman Empire were in Venice, Geneva, Moscow, Marseilles, Nice, and along the northern Black Sea coast.

Like many people throughout history who have been subjugated by another power, there were also secret societies of Greeks within the Ottoman Empire that taught their children and discussed the idea of Greek independence.

One problem facing the men and women thinking about a "free Greece" was they didn't really have an idea of what Greece should be. Outside of what we call Greece today, many Greeks lived in Constantinople and Asia Minor, living with millions of Turks and people of other ethnicities. Even in Greece, especially on the islands near Albania and Turkey, the population was mixed. The population of the coastal mainland, including Athens, which, in 1821, the year the War of Independence began, only contained just less than twenty-four thousand people (today that number is just under eleven million, about one-third of the population), was also a jumble of Greeks, Turks, and others living next to one another to a great degree. The only part of today's Greece that was predominantly Greek was the lower central area and the Peloponnese. The mountainous borderlands contained Greeks, Albanians, Macedonians, Bulgarians, and a small number of Serbs. That left what was readily identifiable as "Greece" as the poorest, most backward part of the country. Hellenism, the idea that the last great Greek civilization existed at the time before Alexander the Great, rose up in Greece and Europe, especially France and England. By looking back to this distant history, Greeks in the 19th century could readily identify areas of the world that had been governed by Greeks, where Greek was spoken as the dominant language, and where Greek culture was dominant. However, looking back to a world that existed nearly two thousand years before did not hold much relevance.

This idea of Hellenism, which contained not only geographic concepts but also ethnic ones, combined with the ideas that had grown with the western European Enlightenment and the French Revolution, primarily the idea of a nation-state, one over which the people (not a sultan, emperor, or king) would govern.

One of the dominant figures of the Greek nationalist movement at the turn of the 18th and 19th centuries was Rhigas Pheraios (Rigas Feraios), who mapped out where the new "Greek Republic" would exist. Pheraios's idea was for Greece to be modeled on the early French Revolutionary governments and consist of what we call Greece today, as well as Constantinople, the entire Aegean coast of Asia Minor (Turkey), and a large slice of the Balkan Peninsula along the Black Sea. Never mind that this was incredibly impractical since millions of other ethnic groups lived in these areas. Despite the impossibility of Pheraios's ideas, the Ottoman authorities hunted him down. He was betrayed by his fellow Greeks and was strangled and thrown into the Danube River.

Rhigas Pheraios.

In 1814, a group of expatriate Greeks in Odesa (part of today's Ukraine) banded together to form the Etairia Philike ("Friendly Brotherhood"), which soon gained followers throughout the Greek community abroad, especially in Russia. Many Greeks joined because they believed that the group was backed by members of the Russian government. What truly spurred this belief on, as well as the growing belief that the tsar himself might actually back an independent

Greece, was the appointment of a Greek from Corfu as the Russian foreign minister.

His name was Ioannis (Anglicized to "John") Kapodistrias (b.1776-d. 1831). Kapodistrias was from an upper-class family and had absorbed the ideas of the Enlightenment and French Revolution in his travels and thorough education. In 1799, Kapodistrias took his father's place in helping to govern the Ionian Islands, which had been jointly set up by the Russians and Turks in their peace agreement. In the course of his career there, he became acquainted with a Russian diplomat stationed in Italy. Kapodistrias became his student and eventually became an ambassador to Switzerland. Finally, in 1814/15, he became the Russian foreign minister.

Despite holding liberal Enlightenment ideas himself, Kapodistrias worked for the decidedly illiberal Russian tsar. Kapodistrias also did not believe that the Greeks were able to govern themselves at that point in time. The Etairia Philike also believed that Greeks should control a new Byzantine Empire, which put them at odds with both Russia and Russia's allies in the Balkans, such as the Bulgarians and Serbs.

Not only was Kapodistrias against any rebellion, but the leaders of the Greek Orthodox Church in Greece were too, as were many of the wealthy merchants of Greece and the Greek islands. Both groups believed a rebellion would bring a massive Turkish backlash, which would not only cost tens of thousands of lives or more but also destroy the economy and the position of the Greek Orthodox Church and its leadership in Greece and the Ottoman Empire.

However, with Kapodistrias in a position of power in the largest Orthodox country in the world, the Greeks of the Etairia Philike came to believe that the time was right for an armed rebellion against Turkish rule. The Etairia Philike enjoyed the most support in the Peloponnese, where the Ottoman rule was weakest. A powerful klepht warlord named Theodoros Kolokotronis, along with Bishop Germanos of Patras and Governor Petros Mavromichalis of the Mani

Peninsula, all threw their support behind the Etairia Philike and the idea of an armed rebellion.

When Kapodistrias told the Etairia Philike in no uncertain terms that he and Russia would not support an armed rebellion, the society approached a Greek from Constantinople who was now in the service of the Russian army, one Alexander Ypsilantis, to lead the rebellion. (Incidentally, Ypsilanti, Michigan, is named in honor of Alexander's brother, Demetrios Ypsilantis, who also took part in the rebellion.)

Unfortunately, Ypsilantis was about as deluded as the members of the Etairia Philike who had fallen in love with their own propaganda of a giant new "Byzantine" Greece. He also believed that the time was right and pushed ahead in an attempt to raise an army in the hinterlands of the Peloponnese and the mountainous regions of Greece. His hope was that he could win the armed support of the Serbs, who had just won their independence from the Turks, and that a few victories would push the Russians and Slavic people of the Balkans to aid the Greeks. None of that would happen. The Serbs had no interest in further warring with the Turks, and the Russians, as has already been shown, were firmly against an armed Greek rebellion.

In the end, however, as has happened so often in history, events outside of the Greeks' control influenced what was to happen in their country next.

In the mountains of southern Albania and northern Epirus (the northeastern part of Greece), a Turkish governor or pasha named Ali had ruled for thirty years. Ali is a common Muslim name, so this man is known to history as Ali of Janina" (in Greek known as Ioannina). Ali's sons ruled the Peloponnese in his name. In essence, Ali was the true ruler of the area, with the sultan being a distant personage who collected taxes.

Ali had proved himself in battle and had proved himself ruthless when faced with rebellion. In 1803, Greeks in the area of Souli in Epirus rose up against Ali's rule. Ali killed virtually all of the men, and many of their widows and children threw themselves off a nearby cliff rather than face capture by Ali's forces. Ali ruled from central Albania south to central-western Greece, and he was powerful and influential enough to summon foreign ministers to his elaborate court.

By 1820, however, Ali was growing too strong and independent-minded for the Ottoman government in Constantinople. The sultan, Mahmud II, declared him an outlaw and sent fifty thousand men to remove Ali from power. This took two years, and while the Ottomans were fighting among themselves, the Greeks of the Etairia Philike decided to make their move, believing that the Turks would not be able to stop their revolution.

Taking the lead was Alexander Ypsilantis, who was in the Russian army and stationed in Moldova. Alexander, along with several other Greek officers serving in the Russian forces, moved south into Turkish territory to begin the Greek Revolution. One of Ypsilanti's men, an officer named Soutsos, informed the Turks of Ypsilantis's intentions, and they began to move forces to intercept Ypsilanti, who had moved into Romania, hoping to encourage the ethnic Greeks and Romanians to revolt against the Turks.

Ypsilantis's entire time in Romania was a fiasco of betrayal, miscalculation, disappointment, and bloodshed. Even before the Turkish forces arrived, Ypsilantis and his men had been excommunicated from the Greek Orthodox Church by the archbishop in Romania for bloodthirsty crimes that took place while Ypsilantis's men were searching for supplies (and plunder). Not only did Ypsilantis's actions result in his excommunication, but they also discouraged any of the Balkan people from rising up against the Turks or helping the Greeks. Even the Russians, who Ypsilantis had hoped would support him, allowed Turkish forces to cross their territory to get to him. At Dragastani in present-day Romania, Ypsilantis and his forces were totally wiped out by the Turks.

Ypsilantis's dream that a Balkan-wide revolt against the Turks would never come to fruition, and his defeat was a humiliating one.

However, no one likes a heroic death in the face of impossible odds more than the Greeks (remember Thermopylae?).

Word spread of Ypsilantis's uprising and defeat in the south, and it lit a fire in Greece, where open warfare soon broke out. Combat between Turks and Greeks, at this point in time, was rarer than the fighting that took place between Greeks. On the one side, there were regions of Greece that had prospered under the stable Ottoman rule and were not eager for the uncertainty of war or the certainty of Ottoman punishment. On the other side, there were the independence-minded Greeks. And within both camps were various factions. When war did break out, many klephtic bands warred against each other because of their respective stands on war against the Ottomans, personal and historic feuds, and/or plunder. Making things worse, as the war went on, the Ottomans were able to bribe certain chieftains to join their side only to see them counter-bribed later and fighting against them once more.

Chapter 4 – The Greek War of Independence

Illustration 2: The Reception of Lord Byron at Missolonghi by Theodoros Vryzakis, 1861. Courtesy National Gallery of Greece.

https://commons.wikimedia.org/wiki/File:Lord_Byron_at_Missolonghi.jpg

The Greek War of Independence began two hundred years ago, as of this writing in 2021. Like many important events in the life of a nation, the painting above, which was completed forty years after the Greek Revolution began, portrays a romantic ideal that many Greeks still adhere to today. Here, we have the various factions of Greek independence represented: the Greek Orthodox Church, the klephts, intellectual- and middle-class Greeks in "modern" European clothing, humble yet brave women kneeling at the feet of the archbishop, and Lord Byron, the Englishman who came to epitomize the Greek War of Independence for many Europeans and Americans. In the painting, Byron is welcomed as the representative of England and other western European powers, which many Greeks thought would rush to their aid.

Like the painting of George Washington crossing the Delaware River during the American Revolution, the painting above bears little resemblance to what actually happened. Byron had the support of many intellectuals in Britain, France, and the United States, but he hardly brought welcome news for the Greeks. Western Europe would not send forces to their aid. Byron spent much of his own money, a sizable sum, in fact, to refit many of the ships of the Greek navy. However, much of Byron's time in Greece was spent writing poems and letters, urging his friends and others in the West to send money to help the Greeks; most of his pleas fell on deaf ears. Byron was also greatly disillusioned by many of the Greek leaders, all of whom competed with and against each other for a share of his sizable checkbook.

In Greece today, the monastery of Ayia, southwest of the city of Patras in the Peloponnese, holds the flag that Archbishop Germanos raised to "signal the revolt" among the Greeks. While Germanos was an early supporter of Greek independence, his gesture was more of a symbolic one, for the war had already broken out throughout much of Greece by the time he raised the flag in late March 1821. Monks in the monasteries near Mount Athos rose in rebellion, and the clans of the Mani Peninsula (the westernmost peninsula of the Peloponnese) had already seized some important towns and Turkish outposts.

The war broke out for a number of reasons. Obviously, the first one was occupation by a foreign power. But the Turks had controlled Greece for centuries, so why rise now? The men of the Etairia Philike had roused the people with propaganda and dreams of a greater Greece ruling from Constantinople, and many believed that Russia, an Orthodox country and the traditional enemy of Turkey, would support a Greek uprising. Many Greeks believed this would be especially true if they managed to win a few victories against the Turks themselves.

Many Greek Orthodox officials (from Archbishop Germanos down to local priests and monks) also encouraged the idea of a rebellion. For the most part, Muslims and Greeks (the overwhelming majority of whom were Orthodox) managed to coexist, but discriminatory laws and behavior on the part of the Turks and the Greeks' belief that the Turks were "infidels" who had to be pushed out of their Christian land always had tempers at a slow boil.

By 1821, the Greeks had also recognized that the Turks were no longer the power they once were. The Serbs had recently won their independence, so why couldn't the Greeks? Of course, the Turks were, at least on paper, much stronger than the Greeks, and Serbia was not worth as much to the Ottomans as Greece.

Even today, Greece and Turkey point fingers at one another for any number of atrocities committed by the other. Nationalists on both sides do not hesitate to bring up incidents from hundreds of years ago as if they happened yesterday. Suffice it to say that there was enough bloodshed on both sides in the history between the two people for both sides to be guilty of a number of what today could only be called "war crimes."

In the Peloponnese, the mainland region farthest from Turkey, Greeks from every part of society rose up to remove the forty thousand or so Turkish residents from the area. It's estimated about half of this number were killed in what today would be called "ethnic cleansing," but the Greeks at the time and since would state that they were reclaiming their homeland for themselves.

Throughout the islands in the western part of the country, rebellions also began. The shipping and naval centers on Hydra, Psara, and Spetses fell to the Greeks, and combined with their already strong position within the Turkish navy, the Greeks gained control of the seas, which made it difficult if not impossible for the Ottomans to reinforce and supply their isolated outposts.

In October, in the city and the area around Tripolitsa, located in the center of the Peloponnesian Peninsula, foreign visitors and consular officials, many of whom, like Byron, held idealistic notions of the Greeks based on the Greek "Golden Age" of ancient times, were stunned to see mobs of Greeks led by clan chieftains and klephts involved in the wholesale killing of over ten thousand Turkish men, women, and children. Also caught up in the carnage were about two hundred Jewish residents of the town; they, too, were killed by the Greeks, who began to see themselves as Christian "holy warriors." Some of the methods of execution included burning and crucifixion.

From the spring to the autumn of 1821, the reaction of Sultan Mahmud II was relatively muted, at least in Greece itself, and gave the Greeks a sense of false hope. Mahmud was actually somewhat of a reformer, and he was between attempts to change entrenched and archaic administrative and governmental practices. He also had to contend with tensions with Persia, Russia, and the tribes of the Arabian Peninsula, so he had much more to deal with than the rebellion in Greece.

Not that Mahmud was idle. On Orthodox Easter Sunday, 1821, the Orthodox patriarch of Constantinople, who was responsible for keeping his Christian subjects in line, was hanged outside of his palace and left there for three days. His body was then cut down, and in a sign of how the sultan ruled by the principle of "divide and conquer," it was given to influential Jewish officials, who then dragged the body to the water of the Golden Horn and threw it in. The Greeks and Jews in Constantinople had competed for centuries for influence and power within the Ottoman Empire, and now, they set upon each other once again.

The hanging of the patriarch was a signal to the Greeks of what would happen should they support the rebellion. Throughout Constantinople and the areas of Turkish Thrace and Asia Minor where large numbers of Greeks lived, the sultan and his officials had hundreds of influential and well-to-do Greeks executed. In Anatolia (today's central Turkey), the town of Kydonies (now Ayvalik), which had been mostly Greek for centuries, was destroyed, and its thirty thousand Greek inhabitants were slaughtered. Upon hearing of the Greek atrocities in the Peloponnese, Turkish reprisals spread and grew more savage. On the islands of Rhodes, Cyprus, and Kos (all relatively far from the Greek mainland and none of them fully sold on the idea of rebellion), thousands of Greeks were put to death.

The most infamous Turkish atrocity of them all was on the island of Chios. At the beginning of the rebellion, most Chiotes were either apathetic or against the rebellion. Part of the reason for this was the location of the island, as it was less than four miles from the Turkish mainland. If the sultan wanted to punish Chios, it would not take long. Second, Chios was one of the richest islands in Greece and a prize possession of the sultan. The island was the center of shipping, trade, and mastic (a gummy pine resin that is in various incense, liquor, gum, and wine—definitely an acquired taste!). The merchants on Chios knew that joining the rebellion would be disastrous for them and likely for most of the people on the island.

However, in the early spring of 1822, a few hundred Greek fighters landed on Chios and attacked the Turkish garrison there. They then forced the Turks into the citadel near the capital (also named Chios). By appealing to the islanders' patriotism and making veiled threats, the Greek rebels gained the support of some Chiotes, but the vast majority remained on the sidelines. After all, along the eastern coast of the island, most of the Chiotes could just look out their window and see Turkey.

On March 22nd, 1822, a large Turkish fleet arrived in the harbor of Chios and seized the city. Eventually, some forty thousand Ottoman troops landed on the island (one for every three inhabitants). On April 12th, orders came for the troops to burn the city of Chios to the ground and to kill all males over twelve, infants, and women over forty. The rest were to be enslaved unless they agreed to convert to Islam. Bags of bones and other remains of the Chiotes were displayed in parts of Constantinople, both as a warning and a victory symbol.

Over the next few months, about ninety thousand Chiotes were killed, died from disease or malnutrition, or were enslaved. Perhaps twenty thousand escaped the island or hid in its central highlands, and it's estimated only about two thousand to five thousand people remained on the island when the war was over. After Greece had won its independence, many people from the island of Crete were encouraged to settle on Chios to help repopulate the island.

Stories of the massacre on Chios spread throughout Greece and Europe, rallying many more to the Greek cause despite the Greeks committing atrocities such as those described above. In 1824, the famous French painter Eugène Delacroix finished his giant painting, *The Massacre at Chios*, which today takes up almost an entire wall at the Louvre Museum in Paris. The painting, seen below, did much to garner support for the Greeks in France.

The Massacre at Chios, Eugène Delacroix, 1824Chios never recovered its former wealth after the massacre, but the events there did inspire many more Greeks to join the rebellion.

https://commons.wikimedia.org/wiki/File:Sc%C3%A8ne_des_massacres_de_Scio,_Eug%C3%A8ne_Delacroix_-_Mus%C3%A9e_du_Louvre_Peintures_INV_3823_-_Q2290433.jpg

At the start of 1822, the sultan's armies moved into mainland Greece. What they seemed most focused on was putting down Ali Pasha's (Ali of Janina's) rebellion in southern Albania and northwestern Greece, but while they were destroying his forces, they put many of the Greek rebels in northern Greece and the Peloponnese to flight. In Salonika in Thrace and in the city of Naousa in central Greece, Turkish massacres of Greeks occurred, as they did in village after village. In some cases, Greek fighters and civilians threw themselves off cliffs to avoid capture by the Turks. What was left of the rebels on mainland Greece fled to the interior of the southern Peloponnese, as they knew they would be facing even more

Ottoman troops once Ali Pasha was defeated, which he was in February. His troops were cornered and besieged, and one among them assassinated Ali and delivered his severed head to the Turkish forces. This was then sent to Constantinople to be put on display to discourage any other ambitious officials.

With Ali Pasha out of the way, the Ottomans could concentrate on the Greeks. They possessed a marked superiority over the Greek forces, who were disorganized, spread out, differed on what path forward to take, and had no real source of income. The Greeks did, however, control the seas, which meant the Turks had to take grueling and narrow coastal roads in order to march on Greek strongholds and to relieve their various fortresses and bases, particularly the one in Athens, which was nearing starvation. Taking to the interior mountains would not have saved much time and would have left the Turks susceptible to the klephts and their guerrilla attacks at which they excelled.

In addition to the Turks' goal of relieving their garrison in Athens, they were also determined to seize Corinth, which made access to the Peloponnese much easier, as well as the town of Missolonghi, which did the same.

The year 1822 started off well for the Turks. Though the garrison in Athens, which was stationed at the Acropolis and had been destroyed by a Venetian barrage in 1687, fell before it could be relieved, the Turks captured the ancient city of Thebes and crossed the Isthmus of Corinth into the Peloponnese, causing a short-lived Greek "government" to flee before them in terror. Many of the klephts fled to the mountains and even debated switching sides.

At the beginning of August, at the citadel of Argos, Alexander Ypsilantis's brother Demetrios (the namesake of Ypsilanti, Michigan, 1793–1832) and a few hundred of his followers held up thousands of Turks under Dramali Pasha before moving out to seek water. Just when the Ottomans could have moved farther into the Peloponnese and perhaps won the war, Dramali Pasha's nerves got the best of him, and he began to move back toward Corinth. Unfortunately for him and the men under his command, he hadn't secured the important and narrow Dervenakia pass leading back to Corinth. There, anywhere between eight and ten thousand klephts and Greek soldiers fell upon the estimated twenty thousand or more Turks, slaughtering most of them. Leading the Greeks were Ypsilantis, and a number of klepht chieftains, the most important and powerful of which was Theodoros Kolokotronis (1770–1843), who later became the head of all the Greek forces in the War of Independence and is a national hero in Greece to this day.

Kolokotronis and other klepht chieftains at Dervenakia.

*https://commons.wikimedia.org/wiki/File:Peytier_-
_Kololotronis_and_his_personal_escort.jpg*

The Greek victory at Dervenakia led to the recapture of Corinth, as well as the important Peloponnesian city of Nauplion (also known as Nafplio).

Ypsilantis, Kolokotronis, and many other men were heroes of the Greek War of Independence, but many women fought, gathered, passed intelligence and weapons, and worked as nurses. The most famous woman of the time was Laskarina Pinotsi, better known to Greeks and history as "Bouboulina"—the feminine version of her second husband's name, the rich shipowner and captain Dimitrios Bouboulis, whose fortune she assumed when he was killed in a battle with pirates. Bouboulina was born in a Turkish prison to a woman from the island of Hydra who had been permitted to see her captive husband. Bouboulina, however, lived much of her adult life on the island of Spetses.

When he was killed, Bouboulina took over his affairs and did much business with Russia, for whom her husband had sailed. The Ottomans tried to seize her property, and she fled to the Russian consulate in Constantinople, from where she was then sent to Crimea. She must have been a woman of great charisma because while at the Russian consulate, she actually met Sultan Mahmud II's mother, who convinced her son to leave Bouboulina's property alone.

Bouboulina had a number of ships built before the war with Turkey broke out, including one which she commanded: the *Agamemnon*.

During the war, Bouboulina and other captains prevented Turkish reinforcements from reaching isolated bases and fortresses and raided Turkish-held lands for weapons and resources. Unfortunately, the Greeks in 1824/25 were not only fighting the Ottomans but fighting each other as well.

Illustration 3: Bouboulina in command on her ship, Agamemnon.

In 1824, Bouboulina was arrested by the nominal Greek government for her support of Kolokotronis, who had been jailed both for not following commands (from a government that barely existed) and for seemingly holding ideas about becoming the "Greek Napoleon." She was released back to her home on the island of Spetses in late 1824, but her family became embroiled in a feud over the elopement of Bouboulina's son and his bride. In patriarchal Greece, a young woman did not get married without her father's permission. An armed group from the girl's family marched to Bouboulina's house, and when she went out on the balcony, she was immediately shot in the forehead and died. No one was ever brought to account for her murder.

After her death, Tsar Alexander I of Russia named her an honorary admiral in the Russian Navy, and in 2018, though she had been regarded as a hero in Greece for centuries by then, she was named the rear admiral of the Hellenic (Greek) Navy.

Fortunately for the Greeks, the Ottoman forces faced considerable problems as well. But despite having sustained a number of defeats at the hands of the Greeks and losing control over many Greek islands, the Greek forces really only controlled a large part of the southern portion of the country—the Peloponnese and the rugged mountains in the center and far north of the country.

However, due to the Greeks' control of the sea, the Turks were forced to march long distances for each campaign, and this could only truly be done in the relatively good weather of late spring and summer. This also forced the Ottomans to plan exceedingly well, something they did not always do, and at this point, Sultan Mahmud II had to deal with large-scale corruption in his forces, mainly in the elite Janissaries.

By this time, the Janissaries were made up of not only men who had been taken from their homes as children but also foreign volunteers and the children of Janissaries. They had grown in size to about 100,000 men at the turn of the century, and they could make or break governments. By this time, they also had to be bribed into fighting in Greece, whether it was with money, gold, jewels, lands, and/or positions.

Though the Turkish forces were fraught with troubles, so were the Greeks, and like the Ottomans, the trouble was of their own making.

In Greece, the rebels were divided into four main factions: Western-thinking Greeks, rich landowners, former Greek Ottoman officials, and the klephts (though among the klephts and landowners, there were factions within factions within factions).

In the early 1800s, the ideals of the French Revolution spread throughout Europe. It was brought to foreign lands by French troops and the writings of the Enlightenment and revolutionary authors. Among the educated and more wealthy Greeks of the diaspora in

Russia, France, Italy, England, and elsewhere, these ideals were the perfect answer to the problems they faced, and since many of the ideas of the Enlightenment were based on modern thoughts on the ancient Greeks, it seemed a perfect fit for a future Greek state.

The wealthy landowners felt differently. They wanted to hold onto their land and influence. Some of them might have been in favor of an English-style bicameral system where they would be members of the Greek "House of Lords," but most of them believed that they should govern. They saw the Greek people as being uneducated and used to authoritarian government, so they thought the common people were not ready for the kind of "freedom" the "Western Greeks" preached.

The klephts sort of blew with the wind, but all of them (meaning their leaders) wanted a say, and since they had done much of the fighting, as opposed to Western-style soldiers raised by other wealthy Greeks, they expected a say in the country's future. In the interim, the klephts raided one another's territory and took what they needed and wanted from poor villagers throughout the country.

In 1824/25, the war was at a stalemate. The Greeks were fighting among themselves and were not strong enough to defeat the Turks on the mainland. The Ottomans were not able to subdue the Greeks and were confronted by the problems described above. The Greeks had hoped that the people of the Balkans and the Russians would help them, but that was a pipe dream. The only hope the Greeks had was to win a stunning victory and show the foreigners that victory was possible or to sustain more of the horrors inflicted on them by the Turks, such as that on Chios.

The sultan needed more forces to retain and regain his Greek territories, and the only way to do that was for him to ask one of his powerful vassals for help. By the 1800s, the power of the sultan was not what it had been. In the 1500s or 1600s, all the sultan had to do was command a vassal, and it would be done. By the 1800s, however, corruption, the rise of powerful administrators, and the ever-present fear of assassination, on top of long distances and the lack of a treasury, meant that Sultan Mahmud II had to call upon his vassal, the powerful Mehmet (Muhammad or Mehmed) Ali of Egypt, for aid. Mehmet was, like Ali of Janina, an Albanian who had risen through the ranks of the Ottoman government. He had established himself as the governor of Egypt, but in actuality, he was its ruler. In order to secure the help of Mehmet Ali, Mahmud II had to promise him the rule over Crete and his eldest son, Ibrahim, the rule over the Peloponnese when the war was over.

In the spring of 1824, the forces under Ibrahim landed in Crete and began marshaling forces for the invasion of the Peloponnese, which occurred about nine months later in January 1825. Now with a powerful naval force and armies both well equipped and trained in Western tactics, Ibrahim's men began to drive deep into the Peloponnese.

Greek infighting had weakened their forces, and the guerrilla tactics that had been previously used against the Turks did not have much effect on Ibrahim's troops and his experienced commanders. The Greeks even released Theodoros Kolokotronis from prison in the hope that he could rally the Greek forces and defeat Ibrahim's armies but to no avail. Throughout their march north, the Ottoman forces conducted a campaign of terror, capturing thousands of Greeks and opening a huge slave market in the city of Modon (Methoni). Elsewhere, entire villages were destroyed, livestock seized, and fields and orchards burned.

The only "bright" spot was at the Battle of the Lerna Mills, which protected the city of Nauplion (the seat of the Greek government, such as it was). There, Demetrios Ypsilantis, along with two other men whose names are familiar to Greeks today, Yannis Makriyannis and Andreas Metaxas, and three hundred soldiers with two gunboats held off an Egyptian/Ottoman force of five thousand, preventing the seizure of the city and the government.

By 1826, the Greeks held just a small part of the northern Peloponnese around Nauplion, the Isthmus of Corinth, and the town of Missolonghi, and they were besieged and isolated in the Acropolis in Athens. It seemed like nothing could save the Greeks from defeat except foreign intervention.

Foreign intervention would come in two forms, but before nations like England became involved in the conflict, some of their citizens, known collectively today as the "Philhellenes" ("those who love Greece and the Greeks"), volunteered to help the Greek cause.

The rise of the Philhellenic movement in Europe was a boon to the Greeks. However, the fact the War of Independence and the Romantic movement happened all at the same time shouldn't be discounted as they all influenced each other. Throughout western Europe, many young men and quite a few wealthy women were attracted to the Greek cause. The struggle of the Greeks and the desire to aid them fit perfectly with the renaissance of learning the Greek classics and antiquity. It also seemed to fit the ideals of the Enlightenment for men to be free and with the Romantic ideals of individualism, emotion, and adventure.

As you read earlier, the most famous of the Philhellenes was George Gordon, Lord Byron, who was already famous in Great Britain for his poetry and wealth and infamous for his many affairs (one of them with his half-sister, which was the immediate cause of his leaving England). In January 1824, Byron arrived in Greece in style. He brought nine servants, an assortment of military uniforms, a personal doctor, and crates of books. Byron was in Greece (at Missolonghi) for a total of three months before succumbing to fever brought on by malaria. In that short time, he worked to try to bring the various Greek factions together to work as one against the Turks. He was not very successful in this, but his fame, his work, and his death, which came at a time when Philhellenism and Romanticism were at their height in Europe, did much to bring attention to the Greeks' plight. Byron is a hero in Greece today, but to be frank, the poet was shocked by the primitive attitudes and cruelty he met among some of the Greek factions.

Statue dedicated to Byron in Athens. Here, Byron is in the arms of a loving Greece.

athenswalk, CC0, via Wikimedia Commons
https://commons.wikimedia.org/wiki/File:Lord_Byron_statue.jpg

Other Europeans had more of a literal effect on the war. Some of them raised money to buy weapons, ships, and equipment for the Greeks, much of which was sent along with volunteers who came from England, France, and Italy. One of the most famous volunteers was British naval officer Frank Dabney Hastings, who had actually joined the Greek navy at the beginning of the struggle and distinguished himself in many battles at sea. Another was Earl Thomas Cochrane, an adventurer who, among many other things, hijacked much of the Brazilian Navy and fought for many Latin American countries in their fight for independence from Spain. Unfortunately, the principal plan of these two British expatriates failed. They wanted to build a modern navy powered by steam. Much of the money was lost to corruption and incompetence. Only one ship, which was built in America, was completed. Others blew apart due to faulty steam engines, and others lay half-built on the Thames in England, victims of bankruptcy.

Despite the Philhellenes' seeming failure, their participation and the news coverage that followed them (much of it a glorified half-truth) caused many of the governments, especially in England and France, to take notice. It also helped that the educated public put great pressure on them to come to the aid of "poor Greece."

Even the tsar in Russia, who had not wanted to involve itself in the conflict, preferring the familiar status quo with the Ottomans, came to believe that he had to do something to protect the Orthodox faith in Greece, where the Turks were destroying churches and killing clergymen. In 1825, the Russians announced they would support the idea of three small Greek territories that would be under the sultan's control while remaining largely autonomous. Though this was progress, it was not what the Greeks wanted.

In England, in 1822, a new government under Prime Minister George Canning had come to power. Although England had originally been against the Greek bid for independence for the same reasons as the Russians (upsetting the status quo and possibly the balance of power in Europe), as the years went by, Canning and many Britons began to show support for the Greeks.

In July of 1825, the Greek government asked the British to make Greece a protectorate, which was rejected by the British since they knew the rest of Europe would object. Still, Canning was working toward achieving peace in Greece and had approached King Charles X of France for help. Together with the Russians, the British and French drew up the Treaty of London, which stated that there should be an autonomous Greek state under the sultan. The borders of this small state would be negotiated when peace came.

Of course, the Ottomans had no interest in this "treaty" that had been written without them; besides that, they were winning. However, that was about to change, for a fleet of English, Russian, and French ships were sent to Greece to prevent the resupply of Ibrahim's army. They were met by a Turkish and Egyptian fleet near Navarino (on the southwest coast of the Peloponnese) on October 20th, 1827. In perhaps the last European battle of sailing ships, the Allied fleet utterly destroyed the Ottoman naval forces.

Over the course of the next two years, a Greek government was slowly put together, and Ioannis Kapodistrias, the former Russian foreign minister, was named president. The war went on, but the outbreak of conflict between Turkey and Russia in 1828 near the Caspian and Black Seas meant that Greece was a lost cause for the Turks. They simply did not have enough manpower to hold off the Greeks, English (Lord Cochrane was one of two English officers that had been put in charge of the Greek war effort, with the agreement of the Greek factions), French, and Russians in Greece and fight a war with Russia in the north at the same time.

Chapter 5 – Small Greece, Big Ideas, and Many Wars

Even as the Greeks were embroiled in their war with the Ottomans, they fought among themselves, sometimes savagely. However, with the increased involvement of the major European powers (England, France, and Russia), the Greeks were forced to come to some kind of solution to their issues, lest the "Great Powers" back out and the Turks take over once again.

In May of 1827, the two Greek assemblies that had formed during the last couple of years managed to put aside their differences long enough to meet, draw up a republican constitution with a president as the chief executive, and name Kapodistrias as president.

Kapodistrias, who had rejected the offer of leading the Greeks in 1820, reluctantly accepted. His experience in government was in Russia, which hardly possessed a representative government, and he personally was authoritarian in style. His first goal was to grow Greece's border as much as possible before the Great Powers imposed a settlement on him and the Ottomans. He wanted to build a unified national army, but he would not have time for that, so he sent bands of klephts to the north and northwest to seize as much territory as possible. None of these offensives was successful.

However, Kapodistrias's ideas about what needed to be done in Greece were spot-on: construct an efficient administrative system and civil service and begin to build a nationwide educational system.

The problem wasn't Kapodistrias's plan; it was Kapodistrias. He had spent the war in Russia and on diplomatic travels. In 1827, he was in Geneva when he got word of his nomination. He was known as a workaholic, but he did not know his native land very well, and he also did not know many of those who had fought in the war. He was perceived as aristocratic, which was not necessarily a bad thing at the time, but his attitude toward many of his countrymen was that of the worst kind of snobbish aristocrat. To him, the major landowners were "Christian Turks." The Phanariots, those Greeks who had been raised in Constantinople and were close to the seat of Ottoman power, were known as the "Children of Satan." The klephts were "robbers," and the "Western Greeks" who prided themselves on being the bearers of Enlightenment and French Revolutionary thoughts and ideals of the French Revolution were "fools." Within a very short time, Kapodistrias alienated virtually all of the factions he needed to complete the war and establish a unified government.

In the end, all of Kapodistrias's efforts came to naught. By 1829, the Great Powers were the ones calling the shots, not the Greek president. Though the powers eventually settled on the idea of a Greek monarchy, which leaned more toward the English model than the Russian, they also began to see Greece as a place to either grow their own power or limit that of the others.

In 1829, the Russians emerged victorious in their war over the Turks, which they felt gave them the right (or at least the power) to dictate much of what went on in Greece. The English, not wishing to see the Russians gain important influence and especially warm-water ports in the Mediterranean, were adamant that the Ionian Islands (those former Venetian islands in the northwest of modern Greece near Albania) would remain under their protection, as well as the coastline opposite them. Knowing a weak Greece would not be able to stop Russian intervention, the British prime minister, the famed Duke of Wellington, who had defeated Napoleon at Waterloo, insisted on making the territory a British protectorate, which it was until 1864.

The Russians exerted pressure on the Turks and had made gains in their war, which had broken out over treaty violations involving the Russians' involvement in the Battle of Navarino. The Russians won territories in the Danube Delta and parts of what is now southern Russian and the Caucasus.

The French hoped that by evacuating Ibrahim's Egyptian army from Greece and taking them home, they would have influence over both the Greeks and the Ottomans.

What all three powers agreed upon was a small Greece that did not threaten the borders of Asia Minor or Constantinople and that Kapodistrias had to go. Kapodistrias had already become highly unpopular because of both his attitude and his prevention of various war leaders to either seize or keep the spoils of war they had gained in the war's last days.

The Great Powers cast about, looking among the royal houses of Europe for a prince who would accept the position of the first "King of Greece." The first royal they offered the position to was Prince Leopold of Saxe-Coburg, who declined on the grounds that the borders of his potential new kingdom were too small (he eventually became King Leopold I of Belgium—hardly a giant country).

The search for a king took on urgency when, at the beginning of October 1831, the klephtic chieftains and brothers Constantine and Georgios Mavromichalis assassinated Kapodistrias on the stairs of a church in Athens. Kapodistrias was shot in the head and stabbed in the heart, and he died instantly. One of the brothers was beaten to death by the nearby crowd, and the other was executed just days later. Despite his unpopularity at the time, Kapodistrias is honored in Greece today, at the very least for his hard work for the newly independent country.

A few months later, the Great Powers, fearing a civil war, made Greece a protectorate until they could find a suitable monarch who was acceptable to both themselves and the Greeks. They eventually settled on Prince Otto, the son of King Ludwig I of Bavaria (Germany was not a united country until 1871 and was divided into many independent states). Otto took the name "Otho" and became Otho I, King of the Greeks.

Unfortunately for Greece, Otho was more of an autocrat than Kapodistrias, and a new constitution created a unicameral legislature over which the king had much power. As king, Otho already had much power, and a popular uprising in 1843 backed by the army left Otho with even more, such as veto power, the power to appoint and fire ministers, and dissolve parliament. However, he was forced by a popular vote of men—women would not get to vote in Greece until 1952—to agree to a bicameral legislature and call elections.

Otho unfortunately also brought in many of his Bavarian subjects and advisers, whose culture and ideas about the role of government differed greatly from those of most Greeks, who, unlike the Germans of the time, valued individual freedoms and rights and were, to say the least, "tax-avoidant." They also resented Otho's place as the head of the Greek Orthodox Church, which put him at odds with not only the people but also the church hierarchy. Making matters worse, Otho placed a large number of Phanariot Greeks in his government. Many saw the Phanariot Greeks as foreigners at best and Turkish stooges at worst.

To be fair, while Otho was not popular, Greek factions, especially the klephts, did not help matters. These bands, meaning their chieftains, were not eager to relinquish their power. Making matters worse, they were often used by politicians and various factions as strongmen to intimidate others, including voters.

Corruption, which had been endemic to the later Ottoman occupation, simply carried over into the newly independent country. The army, in particular, was rife with it, and bribery was almost a necessity for a promotion of any kind, which meant the rich and/or influential and oftentimes the incompetent moved up the ranks.

Corruption, tax evasion, inexperience, and much else prevented Greece from advancing into the 19th century, which was already moving into the Industrial Revolution, especially in Great Britain and the German states. There were no railroads in Greece for quite some time. There were no modern roads, and there was only one real source of export: currants. And that depended on horse and donkey transportation and a shipping fleet that was rapidly declining with the advent of the steam engine. Just to keep itself running, the Greek government went into massive debt, which eventually meant that paying off the interest on that debt consumed money that would have been better spent on infrastructure.

To expect a newly independent nation to move from a relatively primitive (economically speaking) former colony nearly five hundred years old into a modern one in a decade or two was unrealistic. On top of that, the problems mentioned above actually caused many Greeks to move into the prosperous areas of the Ottoman Empire. Constantinople, the coast of Asia Minor, and Egypt had significant and relatively well-off populations of ethnic Greeks within them. Many of the islands that are today part of Greece were, for a considerable time after its independence, still part of the Ottoman Empire. These included the large islands of Crete, Cyprus, and Rhodes, as well as many of the islands in the eastern Aegean, of which the aforementioned Chios is one.

Greek flag: 1822–1978.

https://commons.wikimedia.org/wiki/File:Flag_of_Greece_(1822-1978).svg

The "Megali Idea" (pronounced "meh-gol-li ee-thay-a"), or "Great Idea"

Making things worse was the rise of an idea that would lead Greece into disaster in the early 1920s. As you can see from the map above, the nation that was Greece immediately after the War of Independence was a much smaller version of modern Greece. Much of the mainland and many islands were still controlled by Turkey or warlords ostensibly loyal to them. Many Greeks still lived under Turkish or foreign control in what they considered their homeland. What's more, perhaps a few million ethnic Greeks lived in parts of the Ottoman and Russian Empires that could not, with the possible and ancient exception of the coast of Asia Minor, be considered a part of Greece proper.

Nationalism in Europe was spawned in the French Revolution and its aftermath. Rather than think of themselves as subjects of a monarch, people began to think of themselves in terms of their ethnicity, culture, and language to a much greater degree than previously.

For the Greeks, whose distant ancestors were the focus of a new interest in Europe and America in the 18th and 19th centuries, nationality took on a new meaning. Many Greeks at the time of independence and thereafter began to feel that they were the inheritors of the glories of ancient Greece. It makes sense that they would, as the last time that the Greeks could say they were truly independent and not part of a larger entity was the time of the ancient Greek city-states. Like many nationalists, especially ones in search of an identity after centuries of foreign domination, Greeks looked back to a "Golden Age" when life was as perfect as life on Earth can get. In the case of the Greeks, they literally could look back on what people all over the world called and still call the "Golden Age of Greece," which gave so much to the world.

In the chambers of the Greek parliament, in cafés, the parlors of the well-off, and in the mountain strongholds of the klephts, the idea that all Greeks should be included in the new nation was born. Never mind that the new nation was barely independent, rife with corruption, and under the watchful eyes of the greatest powers in Europe, which included the Ottoman Empire.

Though the "Megali Idea" never really took on the biological aspect of the Nazis in Germany in the 1930s, proponents of it did ignore almost two thousand years of history and assume that all Greeks were direct descendants of the ancient Greeks, which, of course, was not true.

One relative positive to the Megali Idea was that it united many Greeks, at least on one issue, at a time when unity was hard to come by. The idea that the Greeks were inheritors of the ancient Greek ideal did have some positives. One of them was a large building program that expanded the capital city of Athens, and some of the newer buildings, including the building that parliament was housed in, were designed on ancient lines.

Greek students in Greece and in the homes of Greeks in Ottoman lands (and, later, Greeks in the diaspora as far afield as the United States and Australia) were taught about the glories of ancient Greece and the supposed birthright of Greeks to be united under one banner and within the same borders. Unfortunately, a side effect of this was that a "new" version of what was believed to be the ancient Greek language was taught in upper-class homes. This language, called *Katharevousa* ("clean," meaning theoretically free of foreign words), was made the language of the press, religion, and government. The problem was that the majority of Greeks, who did and do speak *demotiko* or "demotic" Greek, did not speak it and did not want to learn it. Even until recent times, the change in language divided Greeks, with some political and socioeconomic factions supporting one or the other. These factions saw each other as "enemies" at times, for example, during the Greek Civil War, which followed WWII, and the military junta of 1967 to 1974 (the end of which ended *Katharevousa* seemingly for good).

The Megali Idea was used by Otho I as a distraction from both his disastrous policies and personal unpopularity in an attempt to unite the Greeks in 1839 when the Greeks of Crete rose up against the Turks and nationalist Greeks attempted to cause trouble in Asia Minor (both were put down harshly by the Ottomans). The same held true in 1854 when the Ottomans, along with the English and French, who were now Turkish allies against Russia in the Crimean War (1853-1856), were distracted in their fight to the north. The badly led and disorganized Hellenic Army invaded European Thrace only to be pushed back by the Ottomans. The British and French then invaded and controlled the major port of Piraeus near Athens and forced Otho to allow them to "supervise" Greek politics and internal affairs for the next few years. The first two Greek adventures attempting to promote the Megali Idea were disasters, and it would get worse in the next century.

It was only Otho's support of the Megali Idea that allowed him to remain on the throne. At home, his rule had become more authoritarian, and economic development had been slow, sporadic, or nonexistent, depending on where in Greece one lived and who one was.

In the 1850s and early 1860s, the independent states of Italy fought with each other and other powers to become a united and politically liberal country, at least for the time. In Greece, students and younger members of the army looked to Italy as a model for what they wanted Greece to be. In 1862, rebellions against Otho and his policies took place throughout Greece, which eventually forced him to abdicate after thirty years of rule.

A popular vote resulted in the replacement of Otho with a grandson of Great Britain's famous Queen Victoria, Prince Alfred, but the other powers of Europe, which were facing an already powerful British Empire, would not allow this, at least not peacefully. Eventually, the kingship was offered to Prince William of Holstein-Sonderburg-Glücksburg (on the German-Danish border—his father would become the king of Denmark the next year). Prince William became George I, King of the Hellenes—this last word is important. It signifies that George wasn't becoming king to the Greeks, those people who lived within the borders of Greece. Rather, he was the king over *all* Greeks; in other words, he was showing his acceptance and support for the Megali Idea.

Under George and in fits and starts throughout the rest of the 1800s, Greece slowly began to establish the makings of a modern state. Railways were laid down, shipping was improved, an economically powerful merchant fleet was built, much land was reclaimed for development, and agricultural techniques were improved. Revisions in the tax code and the way money was spent meant that the debt was eased, and the government was made more effective and responsive, though it was still a far cry from that of England or other western European countries. Still, improvements were made, and generally speaking, the life of many Greeks improved in the latter part of the 1800s.

Unfortunately, the one area that lagged might have been the most important: industry. By the latter part of the 1870s, less than ten thousand people in the country worked in factories, and at the outbreak of WWI for Greece in 1917, there were only about forty thousand. Still, with the help of foreign investment, Piraeus became one of the great ports of Europe, and the opening of the Corinth Canal greatly reduced shipping times from west to east.

By the late 1800s, Greece had shown signs of advancement, and in at least one area—shipping—it was one of the world's leaders. Still, though it seemed to many Greeks to be a positive and a uniting notion, the Megali Idea persisted, and unfortunately, a number of small successes allowed many Greeks to believe that uniting all Greeks (at least in the Mediterranean, the Aegean, and Asia Minor) was a real possibility. In the late 1800s, Greece was torn by factionalism. For the most part, this was limited to politics and did not extend into violence. On the question of Greece's borders and who should be within them, there were three main factions. We've already discussed one of them, the "Megali Idea," which appealed to most Greeks. The opposite of this was the "Mikro Idea" ("mee-kro ee-they-ah"), or, as you can probably guess, "The Small Idea." Proponents of the true Mikro Idea were content, for the time being, on Greece remaining as it was after the War of Independence, believing that the nation should establish itself on a secure footing politically, economically, and militarily before attempting any expansion of its borders. Others believed that Greece should grow but not to the extent of the Megali Idea. They believed that it was possible to identify and form a Greek nation where Greek was and had been the dominant culture and language and Greek Orthodoxy the dominant religion. These people realized, rightly, that any attempt to expand Greece's territory into the Balkans, for example, would be met with great hostility, not only by the people there but also by the Great Powers.

The proponents of the Megali Idea and those who believed in a larger but contained Greece could at least agree that many of the islands of the Aegean should lay within Greece's borders, and the first among those was Crete, the largest island of them all.

The Cretans themselves had rebelled against Ottoman rule periodically throughout the Turkish occupation. There was an uprising during the War of Independence, which was quashed with brutality by the Ottoman forces. From 1829 through 1866, the vast majority of the people of Crete called for *enosis*- ("union") with Greece.

In 1866, a massive uprising began on Crete, calling once again for *enosis*. Not only were many thousands of the island's people demanding union with Greece but so were Greek officers (supposedly against orders but with the knowledge and aid of the Greek government) and soldiers on the Greek mainland. They rallied to the Cretan cause and went to fight the Turks and other Ottoman troops on the island. Philhellenes in Europe and America raised money and even outfitted a warship to aid the Cretans. The Greek government also tried to form a military alliance with the Serbs in order to form a possible second front to both aid the Cretans and perhaps gain territory in Europe at the sultan's expense.

Within Crete, as you can probably imagine, things took a bloody toll, as the island was also home to a significant and wealthy population of Greek Muslims, who mostly lived in the central highlands and ports on both ends of the large island. Crete was one of the very few islands where Greeks had actually converted in any sizable numbers, and during the uprising, the result was not only a political but also a bloody religious war.

However, as it was obvious that at this point in time, Turkey had no intention of relinquishing one of its most important and last remaining outposts in the Mediterranean, the Great Powers once again stepped in and forced the Greek government to stand down. This resulted in not only much bitterness but also the deaths of hundreds of Cretan civilians, as the Ottoman forces went on a rampage at the end of the uprising in 1869. For their part, the Greeks and Cretans were only given a vague promise, which was secured by the Great Powers, that Turkey might one day reform its rule on Crete to allow for more autonomy.

For the rest of the 19th century, both Greeks and Cretans were frustrated in their hopes for both the Megali Idea (or some form of it) and *enosis*. In 1876/77, the Serbs and Montenegrins rose up against the Ottomans in the Balkans, hoping to push the Turks out of the Balkans for good and to enact their own version of the "Megali Idea" by including more Serbs and Montenegrins within their own small borders. At the same time, the Bulgarians rose up against the Turks, and all of these uprisings had support and aid from Russia. In 1877, the Russians had actually declared war against Turkey, and for a short while, it seemed as if they might take Constantinople.

It seemed to the Greeks that the time was right for them to rise up again against the Turks, and uprisings broke out once more in Crete, as well as Thessaly, central Greece, and the mountainous border areas of Epirus. Unfortunately for the Greeks, the Russians were actually supporting the idea of a "Big Bulgaria," which meant that the idea of a Greek nation jutting into the Balkans and along the Black Sea could not happen. The Russians had sided with their ethnic Slavic brothers at the expense of the Greeks, with whom they shared only a religion. Once again, the revolts were put down harshly by the Ottomans.

Fortunately for the Greeks, however, the peace treaty that ended the war between Turkey and Russia was completely unacceptable to the other powers of Europe, which now included a new "Great Power," a united Germany. An international conference in Berlin was called, and the Russians were forced to back down and give up their support of "Big Bulgaria." However, when the Greeks brought up their own ideas about Greece's borders expanding in the north, they were rejected out of hand.

Over the next few years, the position of Turkey in the region, both due to external and internal problems, weakened. In Crete, the Turks did appoint a Greek governor and allowed some matters to be decided by the Cretans.

In 1885, the Bulgarians went against the decisions of the Berlin Conference and declared independence once again, concerned that the growth of Bulgaria might halt Greek ideas of expansion. Greek Prime Minister Theodoros Deligiannis, worried over the fate of Greeks north of Greece's current borders, ordered a mobilization of Greek forces and prepared them to move north into the mountains of the Balkans to secure territory for Greece. Once again, the British, wishing to maintain the balance of power and stability in the region, interfered. This time, they sent a fleet to blockade Greece and forced them to stand down. Interestingly enough, the British fleet was commanded by Prince Alfred, who had turned down the Greek throne just a few years prior.

The Cretans rose again in 1897/98 and proclaimed the Cretan Republic and demanded *enosis* with Greece. Once again, the mainland Greeks whipped themselves into a state of frenzy, and even the usually cautious royal family got caught up in the call for *enosis*. Greek troops crossed the border with Turkey in Thrace, and for a short time, they occupied Turkish European territory. Greek troops also moved into Epirus but were stopped cold in the mountainous region. A Greek fleet under Prince George (the heir apparent) sailed toward Crete, where most Greek volunteers and Cretan rebels were holed up around the area of Chania (or Hania) and the Akrotiri Peninsula on the northwest coast of the island.

The entire campaign was a disaster for Greece. The Turkish troops in the east and west pushed the Greeks back and approached Athens. Once more, the Great Powers of Europe stepped in, and a naval and marine force from six nations bombarded the Cretans on Akrotiri into surrender. By the late 1800s, the international climate in Europe was tense, to say the least, and the Great Powers did not want the constant Greek uprisings to upset the status quo in the region. They proclaimed Crete an international protectorate, made the Greeks give back all Ottoman lands still in their hands (which was little), pay an indemnity to the Ottomans, and accept an international commission to both supervise the Greek economy to prevent runaway national debt and ensure the nation didn't erupt into chaos. This was a humiliation the Greeks would remember, and they still do, especially since it came from their supposed "friends." The Greeks were reminded of this when the financial crises of the 2000s and onward struck them, forcing them into a similar situation.

Another problem confronting the Greeks was the growth of Slavic nationalism on its northern borders. A few years prior to the Cretan uprising, the Turks allowed the Bulgarians to set up a Bulgarian exarchate (a particularly Orthodox word similar to a bishopric) and an exarch (a high official) who had always been Greek. This further unified Slavic people in the Balkans and seemingly put Bulgaria in a position of power.

For the Greeks, their main concern was the region that is today no less of a crisis point—Macedonia. The ancient Greek word *maćedoine* refers to the mixture of peoples in the area: ethnic Greeks, Turks, Jews, Albanians, Vlachs, and Bulgarians, some of whom were one ethnicity by blood and identified as another by custom or religion. When the Turks set the Bulgarians up in their own high Orthodox office, many Greeks worried that Bulgaria would either claim Macedonia or attempt to seize it either openly or in secret. To the Greek mind, this might also allow the Slavic people to encroach further on land that was traditionally dominated by Greeks, especially around the wealthy city of Salonika.

Illustration 4: Modern map, though the dotted lines indicate the historical region of Macedonia.

Aside from the ethnic and religious problem, the question of Macedonia and who would claim it also brought up a historical question that we will return to toward the very end of the book: the question of Alexander the Great, Prince, then King, of Macedon.

Even before the Cretan uprising in 1897/98, the Greek government had funded expeditions of Greek volunteers and klephts to wage a guerrilla war in Macedonia against similar bands of non-Greeks in the region. Between this, the Cretan uprising, the failed campaign against the Turks, and the costs of governing the nation, Greece was broke when the Great Powers stepped in to get their economy (and their seemingly endless military schemes trying to enact the Megali Idea) under control. All of this brought down a relatively popular government led by Prime Minister Charilaos Trikoupis, who at least had been able to tamp down the factionalism that Greece had been beset by since its independence. For a couple of years after the end of the Cretan rebellion, factionalism tore at Greece.

By 1908, the Balkans were the place where many people believed a major war would start. This eventually happened, although it was not in the Greco-Turkish area of the peninsula, which many expected, but far to the north in Sarajevo.

In 1908, the situation in Macedonia and the area around it got so bad that the Great Powers of Europe once again felt they had to step in to keep the peace. In a number of cities of the European part of the Ottoman Empire, French, Italian, Russian, and British troops landed to keep control. By this point in time, the Ottoman Empire was in such decline, especially in Europe, that the Turks had no choice but to submit.

This submission and the constant loss of territory, combined with the corruption of the empire and much else, led to a revolution in Turkey, which was so profound and shocking to the world that it lent part of its name to the English language. This was the Young Turk Revolution of 1908, which brought younger men from the army, politics, and business together in an attempt to reform the Ottoman Empire and make it more of a constitutional monarchy and less of an absolute one. Prior attempts at reform, along with a more liberal constitution, had been promised and ignored, but the Young Turks succeeded in making the sultan a figurehead, placing the country in the hands of a cabal of officers and a new legislature. In 1912, during a losing effort in the First Balkan War, a more serious coup put the Young Turks in charge of all Turkish affairs. It was the beginning of a move toward Germany and Austria-Hungary.

The rise of the Young Turks also gave new life to a movement that had been boiling just below the surface for years—Turkish nationalism. The Young Turks, generally speaking, felt that too much of the empire was governed and/or populated by non-Turkish people, which had caused innumerable problems over the centuries, especially since the 1800s. These nationalist feelings would end up costing both the Ottoman Empire and many of its people, especially the Armenians and Kurds, dearly.

Reform should have been a good thing for many in the empire, but in actuality, the openness of the rebellion brought home the weakness of the Ottoman state, and one of the main concerns of the Young Turks, the loss of territory, actually got worse.

Bulgaria, which had really been independent for some time, declared its nationhood on October 5th, 1908. The next day, the Austro-Hungarian Empire, which had not been a part of the peace-keeping forces in Greece, seized Bosnia-Herzegovina, along with its capital city of Sarajevo. Elsewhere in the empire, various ethnic groups called for a more representative government and autonomy, which were opposed by the Young Turks.

Once again, the Cretans rose in rebellion against the Turks there. This time, the Greek government was struck by paralysis and took no action, which, in the long run, was a good thing, for shortly after their revolt began, the Great Powers forced the Cretans to back down. Both the submission of the Cretans and the paralysis of the Greek government added to the unhappiness and factionalism of Greece.

Within all of this, however, a man who is still revered among many in Greece and in Greek expatriate communities today came to the fore. His name was Eleutherios (pronounced "Ee-lef-teri-ohss") Venizelos (1864–1936), a Cretan who had played a leading part in the uprisings on the island in 1889 and 1897. Tall, with piercing blue eyes and white hair, Venizelos was charismatic and by all accounts an amazing speaker and debater. Even David Lloyd-George of Britain, who had a similar and much greater reputation in European politics during and immediately after WWI, found Venizelos both hard to argue with successfully or resist.

Venizelos in the 1920s.

In 1910, Venizelos became the prime minister of Greece, and over the next four years, he built a sense of unity among Greeks that they had not experienced in recent memory. His Liberal Party had won 80 percent of the vote, which allowed Venizelos to push forward with relative ease. One of Venizelos's first and most popular actions was to install a progressive income tax, which eased the tax burden on the poor. Education became both free and compulsory for elementary students. The civil service installed a system of tenure, which cut down on bribery and the effects of political influence. Formerly harsh laws against unions were reformed, a minimum wage for women and children—sadly, child labor was rampant throughout Europe at this time—was instated, a primitive form of worker's compensation began, and sick pay and pensions for retirees were worked on. The great estates in the north of the country, which were inefficiently run by absentee landlords or former "Turkish Greeks" (Greek families who had become wealthy under Turkish rule), were broken up.

Unfortunately, despite all of his domestic success, Venizelos, like virtually all Greek politicians of the time, at least the ones who wished to succeed, was an adherent of the Megali Idea. This eventually would become his downfall.

The Balkan Wars

The Balkan Wars of 1912 and 1913 had their roots in the war between Turkey and Italy, which began in 1911 over Italian claims to Turkish territory in North Africa and its desire to include Albania within its borders, which at the time ran down the Adriatic coast, opposite mainland Italy. Eventually, Italy won control over most of modern-day Libya and the Dodecanese Islands south of Asia Minor (of which Rhodes is the most famous). This only added to the already huge number of problems in the area, as the region was populated by Greeks.

Not only were the Greeks now concerned about the Italians encroaching on what they believed should be their territory, but they also had reason to believe that the Bulgarians were now attempting to unite the Slavic people of the Balkans in an attempt to seize or control Macedonia and the other lands of the Ottoman Empire in Europe. The king of Bulgaria, Ferdinand, who outrageously claimed Bulgaria was the true inheritor of the Byzantine Empire, not Greece or Russia, signed a defense treaty with Serbia. Part of this treaty called for the division of Macedonia between them, and it excluded Greece.

The more effective collection of taxes had allowed Venizelos to begin reforming the military and purchase modern equipment from overseas. Adventurous soldiers from overseas, including many French and British officers, helped train the Greeks on both land and sea. Other military reforms helped both the nation and the institution.

A trip overseas gained Venizelos and Greece an ally in the British Chancellor of the Exchequer, David Lloyd-George. In just a few years, Britain had begun to move away from the Ottomans since their empire was racked from within and without. In addition, an increasingly powerful Germany had developed close relations with the Young Turks.

With some behind-the-scenes aid from the British, Venizelos was actually able to approach both the Serbians and the Bulgarians about a defense treaty against the Turks, as well as action against them. Even tiny newly independent Montenegro, which had designs on areas of northern Albania, joined in.

The First Balkan War

During the first week of October 1912, the Montenegrins attacked Turkish outposts in northern Albania. In ten days, the Greeks, Serbs, and Bulgarians all joined in against the Turks. Most of the fighting on land was done by the Bulgarians, who believed they could seize Constantinople and place themselves in a position of strength. While their attempts at seizing the ancient city failed, the Turks in Europe were driven back to the small area of Thrace, which they still control today. The Greeks, eager to seize the wealthy and important city of Salonika, which was populated mainly by Jews and Greeks, moved in just before Bulgarian troops and claimed the city as part of Greece, which it has been since. The Greeks also moved into the Epirus region and announced that Crete was now part of Greece, inviting Cretans to the Greek parliament. Greek troops also entered the city of Janina (today's Ioannina), which had been the headquarters of Ali Pasha before and during the War of Independence.

Illustration 5: The surrender of Salonika to Greek forces by the Ottomans, October 26th, 1912.

https://commons.wikimedia.org/wiki/File:Ottomans_surrender_in_Salonique_1912.jpg

Most people at the time knew that with the Turks driven out of most of Europe, another conflict was likely to erupt among the victors, all of which, as has been described above, coveted areas of the Balkan Peninsula. That conflict was not a long time coming.

Although the Greeks had taken Salonika, united finally with Crete, and pushed the Ottomans out of the Janina/Epirus area, they were concerned with the Bulgarian occupation of Thrace and its position threatening both Constantinople and Salonika. The Serbs and Montenegrins were also concerned about the growing strength and size of Bulgaria, and in the north, Romania had designs on contested territories on its border with the Bulgarians.

The Bulgarians, for their part, felt that they had taken the majority of casualties of the first war, which was true, and that they had not gotten their fair share of the spoils. What's more, they recognized that their former "allies" were now actively plotting against them, especially Macedonia.

The Second Balkan War

On June 1ˢᵗ, 1913, the Serbians and Greeks signed an alliance with each other, which provoked an attack by Bulgarian forces on June 29ᵗʰ, which aimed to push the Greeks and Serbs out of Macedonia. At first, the Bulgarians were successful, but with both Greek and Serbian resistance stiffening and long supply lines, the Bulgarians were soon driven back. On July 2ⁿᵈ and 3ʳᵈ, the Serbians and Greeks, respectively, attacked the Bulgarians. The Serbians held Bulgarian troops in the center, and the Greeks began to move around the Bulgarians' left flank, which threatened to completely cut them off from their homeland and reinforcements. Making matters worse, on July 11ᵗʰ, the Romanians in the north declared war on Bulgaria, and the Bulgarians were faced with a two-front war they couldn't hope to win.

The war came to a swift end on August 10ᵗʰ, 1913. The Greeks had gained most of southern Thrace (it would gain more at the end of WWI) and southern Macedonia. Serbia gained the region of Kosovo, which they claim as their homeland and is still a bone of contention today. The Serbs also gained most of northern and central Macedonia. Albania became independent under the rule of a German prince, and Romania gained territory in the north. The results of the Second Balkan War pushed Bulgaria into the arms of Germany during WWI and, oddly, with the Ottoman Empire as well.

Between the time Venizelos first became prime minister and the end of the Second Balkan War, Greece both knew a degree of internal stability and had more success in expanding its borders than it had seen since the end of the War of Independence in 1832.

To many Greeks, this was not good enough. The Megali Idea demanded that *all* Greeks in the region be brought under one flag, and ideally, Constantinople should be Greek as well. With Turkey weakened and many Greeks still living within its borders, the Serbs and Bulgarians dominating the rest of Macedonia, and the Italians occupying the Dodecanese Islands, the most vocal proponents of the "Big Idea" pushed even harder. Venizelos, agreeing, for the most part, with the Megali Idea and knowing that his political life demanded support for it, continued to push and work for a "Greater Greece."

The years from 1910 to 1913 had seen both stability in government and success at war, but that was all about to end.

Chapter 6 – Much Sadness and Turmoil: The First World War and the Greco-Turkish War of 1921–23

Greece was under no obligation to enter the First World War. Indeed, there were great arguments for not joining either side. It seemed highly unlikely that Greece would join the Turks and their German and Austro-Hungarian allies, but on the other hand, Great Britain and France had not exactly been Greece's friends since the end of the War of Independence. In fact, they had taken the Turks' side far more often than they had the Greeks'.

In addition to all of that, in 1913, the popular King George I (originally from Denmark and the grandfather to Prince Philip of England, late husband of Elizabeth II of England) was assassinated by Alexandros Schinas, who shot the king in the back on a royal visit to Salonika, claiming that the king "owed me some money." Schinas was later made out to be a socialist by the press, but he was more than likely to have been mentally disturbed. The Greeks attempted to make lemonade from lemons by claiming that the accession to power by George's son, Constantine I, was a "sign from heaven" that the Greeks were to reclaim the city of the original Constantine, Constantinople.

Constantine I had led the successful Greek seizure of Salonika, known in Greek as "Thessaloniki," but he was more authoritarian in outlook than his father and was much more apt to use his power.

The First World War began in August 1914, and Greece remained neutral. However, Venizelos pushed for Greek entry into the war on the part of the Allied Powers. He believed that, in the end, the Allied Powers of Great Britain, Russia, and France would be victorious.

Venizelos also realized that Greece's position was quite dangerous. In the north, the Bulgarians had allied themselves with Germany and Austria-Hungary. The Serbs were decisively defeated by the Austrians and sent running south toward Albania and the Adriatic coast, which meant there was nothing except mountains between the Central Powers (Germany, Austria-Hungary, Bulgaria, and the Ottoman Empire) and Greece. In the first half of the war, the Turks were busy fighting the Russians and their allies in the Caucasus area, as well as the British and their allies in the Middle East. In 1915, the United Kingdom and Commonwealth troops landed on the Dardanelles, south of Constantinople. This battle eventually ended in disaster for the Allies, but it kept the Turks from attacking Greece.

Additionally, for historical reasons, it was difficult to foresee any alliance that Greece could make that would have included the Ottomans. The best the Central Powers could hope for from Greece was neutrality, which was what King Constantine and many Greek military officers wanted.

Venizelos was aware of all of the reasons why Greece should stay neutral, but he felt that this would be impossible for a number of reasons. Firstly, Greece had a long coastline, and its economy was dependent on the sea, meaning Greece was quite susceptible to both blockades and attacks from the water. With the Greek economy barely functioning, a blockade by the Allies, who were uncontested in the Mediterranean (even more so after Italy joined them in 1915), could quickly starve Greece into submission. An embargo on Greek exports, which were mostly semi-luxury goods not needed by anyone, would also be disastrous. And lastly, of course, the Allies could swiftly dispatch the Greek navy and bombard Greek fortresses, bases, and cities.

Those were the negatives. Venizelos also believed that there were positives to joining the Allies. He fervently believed they would win, and back in 1914, that was still a big question for most. Thus, Venizelos felt that when the time came to discuss and create the post-WWI world, Greece needed to be at the negotiating table. Neutrality would not do that, but actively joining the Allies would. Being part of the victorious alliance might mean that the Greeks might gain those last significant parts of the "Greek nation" included in the Megali Idea: the coast of Asia Minor, the last remaining part of Thrace, which belonged to the Turks and Bulgarians, perhaps the Dodecanese Islands that was then controlled by Italy, and a number of Turkish-controlled islands in the Aegean. Some of Venizelos's supporters even dreamed of Greek control of Constantinople.

Venizelos went as far as to offer control of the Greek army (also known as the Hellenic Army) to the British and make offers of recently won Greek territory in the north to Serbia in exchange for later gains after the war had ended in their favor. When the king and many of the top army brass found out about this, they were outraged.

However, Venizelos's hand was not the strongest, especially if he wanted so much in return. The Greek army was not as strong as it had been before the Balkan Wars, and the Greek navy, while enough to keep the Turks out of Greek waters, was also small. In order for Greece to profit from the peace treaty Venizelos expected would be the Allies to dictate, he sweetened the pot, and this was where much trouble within Greece began. We'll return to that in a moment.

For his part, King Constantine I pushed for neutrality, even though he was secretly in favor of the Central Powers. The king was a powerful political figure, and he had the power of veto in many cases, as well as the ability to order the resignation of the prime minister and call elections.

In June of 1915, the elections in Greece gave Venizelos, his party, and his platform a majority of the votes. Within a very short time after the election, he allowed the retreating Serbian Army to cross the border into Greece and be shipped to safety in Corfu under the shield of the British Royal Navy. He then accepted a plan by the British and French to land troops at Thessaloniki (Salonika) to forestall any Bulgarian or Turkish moves into the area and perhaps launch an offensive into their territory. Under a treaty signed between Greece and the Great Powers in 1833, the British and French had the right to do this, but that did not mean that all Greeks, especially in the military and those close to the king, liked it.

For their part, the Allied Powers made vague offers to Greece about territorial gains after the war, including parts of southern Bulgaria and, most importantly, the coast of Asia Minor, where many ethnic Greeks lived. (Under the Young Turk regime, many ethnic Greeks found that they were becoming more and more persecuted, and this, combined with historical claims on the area and Allied "promises" of territory there, pushed Venizelos and his followers toward the Allies.) In the end, it turns out that the British and French had made similar promises to the Italians: land immediately to the north of Greece, perhaps the Ionian Islands, undisputed control of the Dodecanese, and control of Albania. This all came out after the Greeks had entered the war in 1917, as Vladimir Lenin in Russia gained possession of Allied communications and released them to the world. Back in 1915 and 1916, however, this was all in the future. Between that time period, the Allies took advantage of Venizelos's offer and his popularity among the Greeks to land troops and ships on Crete and other Greek islands in Aegean, take control of a fortress inside Thessaloniki, and destroy a vital communications hub linking north Greece to the south because they feared the Bulgarians might seize it. This was all done without Greek permission. The king and the military, on the other hand, felt that by aligning themselves with the Allies, Greece would perhaps be giving away territory for good, as well as the control of its own army and land, at least for the duration of the war.

Allied troops in Thessaloniki also added to the problem. The British and French soldiers there were quickly given a nickname by the Greeks: "The Gardeners of Thessaloniki." All they seemed to do was dig, not fight.

In 1915 and 1916, the elections were boycotted by Venizelos and his followers, who simply carried on governing, explaining to anyone who would listen that they had already won elections before that showed overwhelming support for their platform. However, as time went by, more Greeks came to resent the attitude of the Allies for all of the reasons mentioned above. In the spring of 1916, the generals in command of the Greek army announced that they would not allow the Serbs on Corfu to move to Thessaloniki, where they were supposed to link with British and French troops. Even worse, from the standpoint of Venizelos and his followers, who were called "Venizelists," there were a number of incidents in the north of Greece where Greek officers had simply evacuated key border points and given them to Bulgarian and German troops. Within Greece in late 1915, many Venizelist officials were purged; in this case, they were removed from their positions and exiled. (Later in Greek history, political purges often took an exceedingly violent turn.)

To Venizelos, this was treason, and he was determined to do something about it. Because of the strength of the pro-German officers, he fled the mainland for his homeland of Crete in October 1916 and announced a new Greek government. Essentially, there were two Greeces. The king enjoyed support in what was known as "pre-1913 Greece," which consisted of its old borders, and "New

Greece," which included many of the islands and territories gained in the wars from 1912 to 1913.

This was the beginning of what is known to Greeks as the National Schism, which pitted authoritarian, right-wing factions, often including the top ranks of the military from colonel on up, and corporations against more liberal factions, which included much of the middle class, poor, and urban population. This "schism" was felt in Greek politics through the 1970s and perhaps beyond.

With the division of Greece and the possibility that the king might join the Central Powers, the Allies acted quickly. In November 1916, the French issued a series of demands to the Greeks. All personnel of the Central Powers in Greece were to be expelled (ambassadors, diplomats, military attachés, journalists, etc.), the Greek navy was to be disarmed, the main north-south railway was to be put under Allied control, and artillery installations were to be given to the Allies.

Constantine I of Greece.

All of this, of course, caused great anger within Greece, even among some supporters of Venizelos. When a sizable British-French force landed at the leading Greek port of Piraeus south of Athens, they were met with fierce Greek resistance. They sustained heavy casualties and were forced back to their ships. In response, the numerous Allied naval ships off the coast began to shell the city and bombard the royal palace in Athens, which was not far away. They then began a blockade of southern Greece and the Peloponnese, which, by January, had impacted Greece's economy and caused mass hunger.

By January 1917, the king had had enough and agreed to the Allies' terms. Royalist army units were ordered to leave Athens and the Peloponnese, and Constantine was pressured to abdicate and leave the country. His second son, Alexander, was made the new king of Greece (his first son, George, was unacceptable to the Allies for pro-German sympathies). Five months later, Eleutherios Venizelos returned with what was called the "Lazarus Parliament" of his followers (named for rising from the political dead).

When Venizelos returned, two things occurred. Greece joined the Allies, and a cycle of political revenge began, which continued far into the 20th century. In response to Constantine I's removal of the Venizelist officials in 1915, the Venizelists removed many royalist officers and officials and sent many of them into exile on Corfu, where they could be prevented from escaping via the British navy.

Greece's entry into WWI was somewhat anti-climactic. In the spring of 1917, Greek troops took part in an offensive in Macedonia that achieved nothing but heavy casualties. It was not until almost a year later, in May 1918, that Greek troops were involved in heavy fighting, this time against the Bulgarians. This offensive restored some pride to a divided Greek army and pushed the Bulgarians back a considerable distance from the Greek border in Thrace. In September, the Greeks, many of whom were from Crete, joined a British force in a fierce battle of attrition against the Bulgarians near Lake Doiran, north of Thessaloniki. After a prolonged battle, the Bulgarians moved out of their positions to avoid being outflanked to the east.

In October 1918, Greek and British troops in Thrace were given orders to march eastward toward Constantinople. This motivated the Greeks, who hoped to retake "their" city after five hundred years of Ottoman rule, but as the Allied forces approached the Turkish border, they received word of the Ottomans' surrender. Now, the only way that Greece could move toward the goals of the Megali Idea was at the conference table at Versailles, France, where the victorious Allies prepared to create a "new" Europe.

Despite the personal popularity of Venizelos among the diplomats at Versailles, especially among the British, whose delegation was led by Venizelos's friend and admirer David Lloyd-George, the Greeks emerged with very little after WWI. Venizelos lobbied anyone who would listen to him, and he was both well armed with "facts," which very clearly skewed in Greece's favor, and persuasion but to no real avail.

Venizelos knew that Greek possession of Constantinople would never happen, but he hoped that an international administration would favor the Greeks. He wanted the return of the Dodecanese Islands to Greece, but Italy kept them. The Italians also began making claims on mainland Turkey, which was in disarray with the fall of the Ottoman regime and the Young Turks that the war engendered.

Other than keeping the Dodecanese and some minor concessions on the Adriatic coast of what is today Croatia, the Italians, who lost hundreds of thousands of men in the war, left Versailles with very little. What's more, the "Big Three" of France, Britain, and the United States had treated Italy as a minor partner, insulting Italy's honor. By April 1919, the Italians were preparing to take matters into their own hands. They walked out of the remaining talks going on in France and sent ships in the direction of the major city of Smyrna (today's Izmir in Turkey), directly opposite the Greek island of Chios and home to a majority Greek population.

This alarmed Venizelos and most Greeks, and he asked the Allies—meaning the British and French—if they would not interfere if Greece landed a force in Smyrna (ostensibly to protect the Greeks from the Italian troops) before the Italians could get there. Not wanting to see an over-powerful Italy in the Mediterranean, they agreed, and before terms of the Greek occupation in Smyrna could be discussed, the Greeks had sent troops to occupy the city and the surrounding area.

The Greco-Turkish War, 1919–1922

With the Greeks in control of part of Asia Minor for the first time in five hundred years, it seemed to many Greeks that the culmination of the Megali Idea was at hand. In France, Venizelos had presented his ideas of the lands in Asia Minor that should be given to Greece, seen in the picture below:

As you can see, Venizelos's plan was quite ambitious. It was also extremely unrealistic. Even on the coast, Greeks were only the majority in the area just south of Smyrna, north to around the town of Ayvali, and a few miles inland. In other places along the coast, Greeks and Turks were relatively evenly balanced, but the farther south and inland one went, the greater the number of Turks and the fewer number of Greeks. Even many adherents of the Megali Idea were skeptical of Venizelos's claims farther inland.

But in August of 1920, the Treaty of Sèvres between the Turks and the Allies gave Greece almost all of what Venizelos had wanted. The Greeks would get Smyrna and a large area around it for five years, at which point a plebiscite would be held, asking the residents which nation they wanted to belong to. And since most residents of the area were Greek, it was pretty obvious what would happen. The Greeks also received the northern coastline of the Sea of Marmara, including the Gallipoli Peninsula, and all of Thrace, pushing the Bulgarians out forever and moving the Greek border up to the historic defensive lines outside Constantinople. On top of that, they obtained two islands at the mouth of the Dardanelles Strait, which Venizelos didn't even mention, and the Dodecanese Islands were to be negotiated on by the Italians and Greeks (the Italians refused, though, and held the islands until after WWII).

Everything seemed to be going Greece's way, but both Venizelos and many Greeks of all political stripes got greedy. Greek troops began to push into the interior of Asia Minor, and the farther they went, the fewer people were Greek. Needless to say, the non-Greeks they ran across were not happy to see them, but at least, at first, things remained reasonably peaceful.

One of the men who were worried about the tenability of the Greek push into Asia Minor was a general named Ioannis Metaxas (1871–1941), the acting chief of staff of the Greek army. Metaxas believed that Greece's position in Asia Minor was altogether indefensible militarily. Any geographic feature that would allow the Greeks to construct a strong defensive line was deep inside Asia Minor, much deeper than the Greeks wanted to go and certainly deeper than the Allies would permit, not to mention the millions of Turks who lived there. The problem was that the Greek majority area was really indefensible. Even if the Greeks could hold Smyrna and its peninsula, which was possible, it would likely cost more in both lives and money than it was worth. But though Metaxas was absolutely correct, at this point in time, euphoria in Greece was at an all-time high, and no one who advocated leaving Asia Minor was listened to.

The Greeks and Venizelos should have because within Turkey, over the course of 1919 to 1920, a new movement led by one of the 20th-century's greatest statesmen was gaining strength. The party was the Republican People's Party, and its leader was Mustafa Kemal, better known to history as Kemal Atatürk ("Kemal, Father of the Turks").

Kemal had risen to fame as a military officer during the Turks' victory over the Allies at the Battle of Gallipoli. At a point when Turkish fortunes were low, Kemal ordered his men to seize an Allied strongpoint, the capture of which could change the course of the battle. The last phrase of his order is still famous in Turkey: "I am not ordering you to fight. I am ordering you to die." This inflamed the Muslim Turks, and they swept the position of the Allied troops and eventually won the battle.

Since the end of the war, Kemal and his growing number of followers had proclaimed the former Ottoman regime illegal. To them, it was a betrayal of the Turkish people, and they called for a new nation of Turks for Turks. By late 1919, Kemal was in a position to meet with the Allies, and he informed them that all treaties signed by the former Ottoman Empire or the Young Turks were null and void. He would decide what constituted Turkey, not them.

Atatürk in the 1920s

Naturally, the Allies did not take kindly to this and attempted to blockade Constantinople, which included Greek ships. Atatürk simply moved the capital to a new location, a small city named Ankara in the central part of Asia Minor, which is still the capital of Turkey today. To get to Kemal, the Allies were going to have to invade the Turkish mainland, something that none of them was willing to do. As a matter of fact, it was around this point that the Allies realized that Kemal and his movement weren't going anywhere. After Kemal's defeat of a French force that had been left in a small part of Turkey at the end of the war, the Allies began to negotiate slowly with the new Turkish leader. This left Greece and the Greek troops in Turkey extremely isolated.

Venizelos was at the height of his power in the fall of 1920 when things began to go wrong. First, the king, Alexander I, was bitten by a pet monkey. He developed blood poisoning and died. The king had been firmly under Venizelos's control. His death was unfortunate because, with the seeming success of the Megali Idea, politics in Greece had become slightly less rancorous. With his death, those against Venizelos called for the return of Constantine I from exile. An election was held in November 1920, which was essentially a referendum on Constantine. Venizelos surprisingly lost. The issue of the king's return and the high taxes and costs of WWI had left the Greek economy in trouble.

Venizelos went into exile in Paris, and Constantine returned in December 1920. The memory of both his not-so-secret pro-German stance in WWI and the killing of French and British troops at Piraeus was fresh in the minds of the Allied Powers, which by this time were beginning to worry more about the rise of communism and the Soviet Union than the concerns of Greece. Among them was Winston Churchill, who had been the first lord of the admiralty during the first part of WWI, then the minister of munitions, and was chancellor of the exchequer by December 1920. He argued that a strong Turkey, Russia's historical enemy, would be a bulwark against Soviet expansion. Greece's position got weaker by the day.

Seeing the writing on the wall and hoping to gain some leverage at future negotiations, the new Greek government launched an assault against the new Turkish capital, Ankara, in March 1921. Although they fought bravely and effectively, the Turkish position was simply too strong for the Greek forces to break through. A Turkish counterattack pushed the Greeks back to their starting point, where things remained at a stalemate until the next year.

On August 26th, 1922, the Turks launched a massive counterattack, which began to push the Greeks back toward Smyrna. As they advanced, they found evidence that the Greeks had committed atrocities against the population, which was true. As the Turkish position strengthened and Kemal's government became more popular, more Muslims rose up behind Greek lines, provoking a harsh response from the Greeks. Naturally, especially as the Turks advanced, most Greek soldiers who were taken prisoner or trapped behind the lines could expect harsh treatment in return. Though many Greek prisoners were eventually repatriated, thousands more were killed in executions.

By September, the Greeks asked the Allies to interfere. They hoped that they could at least get the Allies' promises for the protection of the Greeks in the area around Smyrna and elsewhere, but their pleas fell on deaf ears. The Turks were winning, and they weren't about to stop until the Greeks were gone from Asia Minor—now Turkey—for good.

The Turkish attack on Smyrna came at a great human cost. Thousands of Greek refugees flooded into the city from surrounding areas. Between the shelling and food shortages, casualties ran high. When the Turks entered the city and its immediate surroundings, massacres of Greeks took place. Within Smyrna, panicked crowds swarmed the docks and piers, hoping to get aboard a ship. Some Allied ships did pick up people in the water; according to survivors, these were mostly French. Others simply steamed away. Many hundreds drowned. Those who could not leave were killed. Hundreds of thousands of "Turkish Greeks" did manage to make it to Greece, where their assimilation proved another great challenge to the Greek government.

Correspondingly, Turks who still lived in Greece were forcibly expelled from the country. So, as the Turks were sealing their control of Smyrna, approximately one million "Greek Turks" were being expelled from Greece, and given the temper of the time, atrocities occurred more often than the Greeks care to admit even to this day.

The Greco-Turkish War of 1919–1922 was a horrific experience for both sides. Estimates of Greek civilian deaths run from 300,000 to 750,000; the lower number is probably closer. It is not known how many Turks were killed by Greeks, but it is likely it runs at least 100,000 or more.

Chapter 7 – Yet More Chaos and Another World War

The Turkish expulsion of the Greek army and the removal of the Greek population of Asia Minor through death or forcible expulsion brought the Megali Idea to an end, seemingly for good. Most Greeks at this point realized that the "Idea" had been and probably always was a pipe dream and that modern Greece, far from being a new power in the region, was simply a small and relatively poor and backward state in a Europe dominated by the Western powers.

At the end of the war with Turkey, Greece was in shambles. The army had been terribly beaten. The economy was barely functioning, and it now had to absorb hundreds of thousands of refugees. The political life of Greece had split between right and left with the National Schism, and this would continue until late in the century.

Between 1923 and 1936, when a fascist-style regime under General Metaxas took power, Greece suffered through a near civil war, the making and unmaking of governments, and, along with everyone else in Europe and much of the world, the Great Depression, which began in 1929.

Even before the ascension of Metaxas in 1936, Greece experienced a brief military government between 1922 and 1924. In

1924, even as the military attempted to intimidate the populace, an election was held that overwhelmingly called for the next Greek government to be a republic. Despite their defeat in 1926, the military interference in government that began in 1922 continued off and on until 1974.

Venizelos became the prime minister again in 1928, and the programs he set in motion might have had a greater effect in another time. He introduced a massive land reclamation project and a series of reforms intended to expand agricultural production, encouraged the purchase of new grain types from America and Canada to increase yields, helped farmers with low-interest loans, and introduced a program of practical education since Greece was short of engineers, scientists, machinists, and others that would bring the country into the 20th century, especially outside of Athens.

One of the more interesting aspects of Venizelos's later prime ministership was his determination to build a respectful relationship with Turkey. And remarkably, throughout the 1920s and 1930s, the Greeks and Turks were able to sign a number of trade agreements and diplomatic treaties.

Unfortunately for Venizelos and many other world leaders, the Great Depression happened in the fall of 1929. It hit Greece particularly hard, as most of its foreign exports were still semi-luxury products, like currants, olives, and mastic, all things that countries stopped importing almost immediately. A significant chunk of the people in the country relied on money sent from Greek emigrants overseas to supplement their income or, in many cases, keep them from going hungry. Since the Depression was worldwide, these remittances almost disappeared. Worst of all, like many countries, Greece began to default on foreign loans.

Within Greece, Venizelos and his supporters kept the bureaucratic jobs for themselves and made sure that supporters of the former military regimes were kept out of the military. These actions, which were just another step in a series of actions and reactions, kept Greece at war with itself.

The Depression spurred the rise of the Greek Communist Party ("KKE"), and although it was still small, it grew during these hard times. Along with the communists, there were social democratic parties modeled on those in Germany, France, and England. Despite their relatively small numbers, Venizelos and successive Greek government leaders persecuted known and suspected communists and socialists, which would lead to a reckoning during and after WWII.

From 1933 to 1936, Greece was racked by political violence. On the one side were right-wing monarchists. On the other were the liberals who supported Venizelos. Then there was the military. An assortment of small parties threw their lot in where necessary to achieve some sort of political gain. In 1933, Venizelos attempted to include the smaller parties in his government to broaden support for his programs, but the situation was so bad that no unity could be achieved. In March, one of Venizelos's supporters in the military attempted a coup, which the old politician tacitly supported.

As a result of this failed coup, a political foe of Venizelos, Panagis Tsaldaris, became the prime minister. However, his time in office was to be short. The monarchists, who sought to replace the republic with an absolute monarchy, became violent. An attempt was made on Venizelos's life, and in response, he and his supporters used violence in return.

On March 1ˢᵗ, 1935, Venizelos and his supporters revolted against the government. This was defeated by the government and military, and Venizelos fled to Paris, where he died in exile almost exactly one year later.

With Venizelos gone and many of his followers rounded up, put on trial, imprisoned, and oftentimes executed, Greece entered a new phase. Tsaldaris was not able to rule effectively, as one of the reforms introduced by the monarchists was proportional representation.

Tsaldaris was not able to build the needed consensus—at least not without the small KKE, and that was something both the military and the monarchists would not accept. The deputy chief of the General Staff of the Hellenic Army, Alexander Papagos, who would command the army in WWII, proclaimed that the army would not allow communists to be a part of the government. At this point in time, the king, George II, who had been unacceptable to the Great Powers before WWI, named former chief of staff Ioannis Metaxas as the prime minister, and with that, the Greek experiment with democracy ended.

Metaxas in the late 1930s.

The Metaxas Dictatorship

Metaxas was born in the city of Ithaca in 1871. He joined the army at a young age and distinguished himself despite the Greek defeat in the war with the Ottomans in 1897. He then went to Germany for advanced training; at the time, many foreign army officers trained in

Germany, as it was considered the finest in Europe if not the world. Metaxas's rise was rapid, and he played a significant role in the Greek planning in the Balkan Wars. Despite his rank of colonel, he was appointed chief of staff in 1913 and was made a general in 1916. Like many monarchists, he was exiled to Corfu during the war, but he returned to Greece in 1920 when Constantine was reinstated after the death of his son from the infamous monkey bite.

Along with the monarchist politicians before and during the first part of WWI, Metaxas pressed for Greek neutrality, and as you read earlier, he opposed Venizelos's and others' plans for the Greek occupation of Asia Minor. In 1928, he was a minister without portfolio in the government. During the first years of the Great Depression, Metaxas strongly supported the monarchy and was the head of a small royalist party when the king appointed him the new commander in chief of the military.

Though it was clear to many that a dictatorship was a very real possibility, no one could put together a coalition to either to govern or preempt the placement of Metaxas as the prime minister by the king on April 13th, 1936. On the same day, under not-so-veiled threats from the military, the Greek parliament voted overwhelmingly to end its own existence.

The only group to oppose the rise of Metaxas, whose only support came from the king (he was not a popular nor charismatic man), were the communists, who announced a general strike on May Day (May 1st) 1936. This gave Metaxas, the king, and the military, who were all extreme anti-communists, an excuse to clamp down. They decreed the censorship of the press, suspended many rights that were "guaranteed" by the constitution, and announced that parliament would not meet again until sometime in the unknown future.

Metaxas is a hero to many Greeks today, but that is not because of his policies during his time in power. Metaxas was a fascist, plain and simple. He modeled much of his regime on the same type of symbols as Benito Mussolini and Adolf Hitler, though, to his credit, he did not practice or initiate any sort of ethnic prejudice or persecution against the Jews or other minorities of Greece. However, he did champion "Greek Civilization" as the cornerstone of modern Western culture and announced the arrival of what he called the "Third Greek Civilization" (the ancients, the Byzantines, and 1936, respectively).

Metaxas was rabidly anti-communist, as were his followers, though, at this point in time, most Greeks had barely heard of communism and likely could not have described it in any great detail. Although he did not practice racial politics as Hitler did, his time in Germany did make him an admirer of that culture, and he wished to install what he deemed a more "disciplined, purposeful and Germanic" ethos into the Greek culture in the hope of making it more efficient, among other things. Like Hitler and Mussolini, Metaxas organized a movement for the young that was literally called the "Youth Movement" and set about censoring schoolbooks and curricula for any sign of liberalism or communism. He even called himself the "First Peasant," "First Worker," and, of course, "Leader."

As you can probably imagine, civil rights within the country suffered greatly under Metaxas, and many were thrown into prison for supposed "communist sympathies," which included protection of workers and farmers against abuse by industrialists and large landowners. Though Metaxas decreed a minimum wage for the first time in Greek history and canceled peasants' debt, these were mostly for public appearance, and these and many other programs supposedly in favor of the poor of Greece were only honored *if* the powerful chose to do so. Naturally, this drove more people into the arms of the KKE or at least made them sympathize with communist ideals, but anyone expressing these was punished severely.

Though Greece enjoyed some stability under Metaxas, it was, of course, imposed. His programs benefited the wealthy as opposed to the poor (there was only a relatively small middle class in the country). The economy moved forward in fits and starts as the Depression continued into 1940—and that's when Metaxas's reputation was saved.

By the fall of 1940, WWII in Europe had been going on for a year. Hitler was the master of the Continent from the Atlantic to the Arctic Circle in Norway to the border of the Soviet Union, which he was preparing to attack in the spring. In North Africa, the war was going badly for the Italian forces under Mussolini, whose reputation as a "tough guy" was suffering both from Hitler's successes and the lack of his own. In April 1939, Mussolini invaded the small nation of Albania, opposite Italy on the Adriatic Sea. He hoped that success in North Africa and the Balkans might help him establish a new "Roman Empire," with him as Caesar.

One of the prerequisites in becoming a new Caesar was control of the Mediterranean. In 1940, the Italians boasted quite a strong navy and were competing with the British for control of the sea. To further his naval goals and grow his empire, Mussolini drew up a series of demands, which were presented to Metaxas during the night/early morning of October 28th, 1940. Mussolini wished to march and land his troops at various strategic points throughout Greece in order to "protect them" from the British, whom the Greeks were leaning toward in their neutrality.

Metaxas had attended a friendly reception at the Italian consulate earlier in the evening where nothing but good wishes were announced by the Italians toward the Greeks, but now, sick and awakened in the middle of the night and dressed in a nightshirt, robe, and slippers, the Greek leader was given a note by the Italian ambassador, Emanuele Grazzi, which, though in flowery and polite diplomatic language, demanded the right to march through Greece and for Italy to take possession of numerous sites on the Greek coast. What happened next is a legend in Greece; in fact, an entire holiday is based on it. According to Metaxas's widow and others, the Greek dictator simply uttered a firm "No!" and had the Italian escorted out. Others who were there reported that the conversation, which took place in French since it was the language of diplomacy at the time, simply ended with Metaxas saying, "Then it is war!"

Either way, the message to the Italians couldn't be clearer—Greece would fight. Every year on October 28th, Greeks celebrate the *Epéteios tou Óchi* (the "Anniversary of the No") or Oxi (Ochi) Day.

For Mussolini, the invasion of Greece, which he launched the same day, was a horrendous failure and humiliation. Not only was the timing of the operation poor, which took place in the late fall during the rainy season, but his troops, like many Italian troops throughout WWII, were poorly trained and poorly motivated. Hitler was not informed about this; it was said he was enraged about being left of the loop, and he correctly feared the Italian operation might affect his planning for the invasion of the USSR (the Soviet Union).

The Greeks, on the other hand, were united, as most people would be when their land is invaded. After a fierce fight against the stronger Italian forces, the Greeks began to push the Italians back into Albania. By December, important Albanian ports were seized by the Greeks, and the Italians, at threat of being cut off before winter weather hit, ground things to a halt.

Unfortunately for the Greeks, their success meant that Hitler, who was always strangely loyal to Mussolini, was going to come to his ally's aid. Another factor was the position of the Greeks vis-à-vis Great Britain, which now saw Greece as an ally. The British pushed Metaxas to allow British troops to take positions in Greece, which he refused, still hoping Hitler might be dissuaded from invading his country. However, Metaxas died suddenly from a burst internal abscess and the blood poisoning it caused. His successor, General Papagos, agreed to British requests, believing a German-Italian invasion was coming no matter what.

The British and Greeks were not able to come to an understanding about defensive plans, which was mostly due to difficulties in language and communications systems, so when the Germans and Italians invaded Greece and Yugoslavia on April 6th, 1941, they put up an uncoordinated defense. At best, the Anglo-Greek force might have held up the Axis longer than they did, forestalling Hitler's other plans, but as soon as the Germans got involved, an Allied defeat was a foregone conclusion.

A number of Greek units in the north surrendered to the Germans, and one of their officers, General Tsolakoglou, eventually became the head of a German puppet regime in Greece. A number of Greek troops and about fifty thousand British Imperial troops (mostly New Zealanders) made their way to Crete, where on April 26th, they were subjected to the last German parachute attack of the war. Though the Germans quickly took Crete, the fight was much more costly than Hitler had imagined. In quite a few instances, German airborne troops, whose weapons were dropped in canisters that they had to retrieve upon landing, were literally beaten to death and, in some cases, torn apart by Cretan peasants before they could arm themselves. Of course, German retribution was swift, and hundreds of Cretans were killed in reprisals. Throughout the war, the Cretans, aided by the British, kept up an active resistance to the occupation.

By the beginning of June, all of Greece was occupied by the Axis, which included Bulgaria. Greece was divided into occupation zones, with the Germans controlling major cities, ports, certain islands, and strategic passes linking Greece with Yugoslavia and beyond as they deemed necessary throughout the war. The Italians controlled most of the country, and the Bulgarians oversaw their former territory in Thrace.

The Triple Occupation of Greece by the Axis Powers (1941-1944)

Legend:
- German Occupation Zone
- Italian Occupation Zone (occ. by Germany after Sept. 1943)
- Bulgarian Occupation Zone
- Bulgarian occupation (under German control) from July 1943
- Dodecanese Islands (Italian possession since 1912)

Cplakidas, CC BY-SA 3.0 <http://creativecommons.org/licenses/by-sa/3.0/>, via Wikimedia Commons https://commons.wikimedia.org/wiki/File:Triple_Occupation_of_Greece.png

Historically, the consensus has been that in a horrible situation, the Italians were less horrible (though recent studies have begun to refute that), the Bulgarians worse, and, of course, the Germans worst of all. Throughout the war, any acts of resistance or attacks on occupation troops, especially Bulgarians or Germans, almost always led to reprisal killings, and many Greeks who had been imprisoned for minor offenses knew that they might be facing a death sentence when the next reprisal occurred.

Throughout Greece but especially in Thessaloniki, which was still more than half Jewish in population, the Germans began their persecutions. This happened in the Italian and Bulgarian zones too, with Greek Jews being handed over to the Nazis. Within weeks, the Jewish population of Greece almost completely ceased to exist.

The Axis forces sent much of the food grown in Greece to their own homes or troops, and within a short time, hunger began to grip Greece. Throughout the war, thousands upon thousands of Greeks died from hunger or weakened immune systems. In the middle of the war, the Red Cross petitioned the Axis to allow aid packages to come into Greece, but outside of the cities, this did not have much effect. An exodus from the cities began as Greeks attempted to find food in the countryside or with families on farms in the interior. On the islands, it was particularly bad, and fishing fleets were tightly controlled.

The Resistance

After the war, successive Greek governments, virtually all of whom leaned far to the right, attempted to downplay the role of the largest resistance group that existed in Greece during the war. They successfully marginalized them as being 100 percent communist and taking orders directly from Moscow.

This group, the National Popular Liberation Army, was known by its Greek acronym of "ELAS." Throughout most of the war, it was made up of not only communists but also republicans, socialists, and patriots of all stripes who simply wished to help end the occupation of their land. Another group, the National Liberation Front or "EAM," often worked with ELAS, and the two were almost always lumped together in both speech and history books. In fact, they still are known as "ELAS/EAM" today. EAM was a smaller and more radical group, and it did have ideas about the communist reshaping of Greece after the war.

ELAS/EAM was by far the largest of the Greek resistance groups, though a smaller right-wing group called the National Republican Greek Army ("EDES") did get a large share of publicity due to its monarchist beliefs and its colorful leader, Napoleon Zervas.

Like many other nations conquered by the Axis, the occupation engendered not only resistance but also civil war and collaboration (in Greece, by the fascist "X" militia). During WWII, it seemed to many

Greeks that the resistance spent as much time fighting each other as they did the Germans, Italians, and Bulgarians.

However, the resistance and the needs of the occupation did require that hundreds of thousands of Axis troops be stationed in Greece. Organizing fights in the mountains and running secret printing presses and intelligence-gathering operations meant that the occupation forces could not fight elsewhere. The most spectacular and effective action of the Greek resistance during the war came on November 25th, 1942, when ELAS and EDES, along with British agents, cooperated to blow up the crucial Gorgopotamos railway viaduct in northern Greece, which cut German supply lines south and had a serious effect on the German campaign in North Africa.

By late 1943, the Greeks and nearly everyone else in Europe, with the possible exception of Hitler, knew that the war was going to end with an Ally victory. Despite the Italians dropping out of the war and the Germans occupying Greek zones and installing their harsh regime, the Greek resistance movements began to increasingly fight among themselves, jockeying for positions when the war ended.

When the war did end, a new round of violence began. Toward the end of the war, British Prime Minister Winston Churchill went to Moscow on his own and met Soviet leader Josef Stalin. During this meeting, Churchill took out a scrap of paper and wrote down the names of various countries in eastern Europe and the Balkans. Next to each, he wrote what he deemed the percentage of control that the Soviets and the Western Allies (meaning Britain and the United States of America) were to have in each. Next to Greece, which he considered vital for the security of the Suez Canal that Britain controlled, he wrote "90%." To this and to all of the proposals made by Churchill, Stalin put a large checkmark in agreement. The post-war world was made. Throughout the rest of his life, Stalin, who was not really known for keeping his word, kept to his part of the bargain in regards to Greece, probably knowing that a naval battle against the United Kingdom and the United States would go badly for him since his power was based on land. Greece and the Black Sea could be easily blockaded by the west.

This left Britain ostensibly "in charge" of what happened in Greece after the war or rather once the Axis Powers left, which happened in October 1944. Churchill was virulently anti-communist, and despite being told that aside from EAM, much of the Greek resistance was not communist, though they might lean toward the left, he believed that any group not supporting the return of the king (who was unpopular) and some sort of republican government under him was a communist.

King George and General Papagos spent much of the war being moved from one place to another, attempting more to wage war against the communists than fight the Germans, though sizable contingents of Greek troops fought in North Africa and Italy. They also whispered in Churchill's ear and inflated the risk of communism in Greece.

The next years of Greek history were spent in a civil war. In 1944, the British landed troops in Athens and installed the king and Papagos. ELAS/EAM, which by then numbered nearly 100,000 men and women, set up a rival government in the north and ran much of the countryside.

On December 3rd, 1944, a huge demonstration against the government and the British took place in Athens. Violence ensued, and British troops fired into the crowd. The protestors claimed hundreds had been shot and/or killed; the number is far less, though it is still tragic. Civil war broke out in Athens between ELAS/EAM, the British, the formerly fascist Greek militia, and some units of the Greek army. In Athens, ELAS was driven out, and mass killings of ELAS prisoners were carried out on the outskirts of the city by members of EDES and the king's government. However, the only parts of Greece under the control of the government and Britain were Athens and Thessaloniki.

For the next two months, battles went on between the government and ELAS/EAM in Athens. However, with much of the city in ruins and no one making any real advances, both sides took part in negotiations sponsored by Great Britain. These negotiations resulted in the Varkiza Agreement of February 1945. Throughout the negotiations, the Greek king remained in exile, and the British-supported prime minister resigned. Both sides needed to make peace. ELAS, now somewhat divorced from the more radical EAM, needed Athens to govern and was eager to avoid the threat of a British blockade. The British were becoming aware that the end of the war and the occupation and administration of Greece and other formerly occupied countries were more expensive than they could afford.

The Varkiza Agreement, named after the town where the talks took place, called for the restoration of civil rights, a plebiscite on the monarchy, and a general election under Allied supervision. These were the demands of ELAS. General Nikolaos Plastiras vowed that he would jail and try all accused collaborators, grant national amnesty for ELAS fighters, and promised there would be no attempt by the army to go after left-wing organizations (like unions) or political parties. ELAS was also required to give up its arms and withdraw its troops 150 miles from Athens.

The Varkiza Agreement, which was signed by both sides, never came into effect. While most ELAS units gave up their arms, some remained in the mountains and small towns and villages of Greece, believing the government would not live up to its promises, which it did not.

Within a very short time, the army moved against ELAS, unions, and anyone else deemed a communist or leftist. Many completely non-political people were also arrested for allegedly having "communist" beliefs. Worse, many former collaborators and the former fascist militia was armed and sent after ELAS/EAM members throughout the country. Rigged elections in 1946 put former Prime Minister Tsaldaris back in power, and he proved to be even more conservative than he had previously been. In September 1945, after a series of rigged elections, King George II returned to Greece as a figurehead.

By 1946, a full-scale guerrilla war was taking place in Greece. By the middle of the year, the British unilaterally announced that they were leaving Greece and that the Americans had better step in, which they did. President Harry Truman announced his Truman Doctrine, which, simply put, stated that any nation resisting communism would have the help of the United States. The first two countries to receive aid were Greece and Turkey, the latter of which the US saw as the more important partner since it bordered the Soviet Union. The US never sent troops to Greece, though political and military advisers did aid the government.

The Americans also pumped massive amounts of economic and military aid into the country. Even with the financial help of the Americans, the Greek Civil War lasted until 1949, though by early 1948, ELAS and the communists were limited to an area bordering Albania and the new country of Yugoslavia. In October 1949, the communists announced the end of their struggle. Many of them fled to Albania and Yugoslavia, where many of them lived until amnesty was declared in the 1980s.

The Greek Civil War of 1947–49 was vicious, as most civil wars are. Both sides were guilty of the most heinous crimes: torture, mass killings, mass imprisonment, the intentional starvation of areas opposed to them, and even the kidnapping of children for indoctrination. The scars of the Civil War lasted a very, very long time.

Chapter 8 – Greece from 1950

Relatively speaking, Greece in the 1950s was stable, and for a short time, its economic growth actually outpaced that of other post-war European countries, though it must be admitted that these nations had seen much greater destruction during WWII than Greece.

There were two main characteristics of the Greek political scene between 1950 and 1967: communism and its cousin, socialism. These parties would not be permitted political power, and the military would play a significant role in the political life of the country. Stability seemed to come to the country, and Greece, along with Turkey, became part of the North Atlantic Treaty Organization (NATO) for the defense of western Europe against the USSR. Even violent anti-Greek riots in Istanbul (formerly Constantinople) did not cause the two nations to go to war, which was seen by many as not only a sign of stability but also a miracle.

However, below the surface, tensions still existed in Greek society. Simply speaking, this placed more liberal-leaning republican governments against the army, the king (Paul II until 1963, then his son Constantine II until 1973) against the military (in the case of Paul) as well as against the left, and the left against right-wing parties and the idea of a monarchy.

On top of all the political infighting, the 1960s saw the same types of changes to Greek society that happened elsewhere in the Western world. One of the by-products of this was growing anti-Americanism, which led to large protests against both the Americans, who had established naval bases in Greece, and governments that supported it. Additionally, the culture wars that broke out as a result of the changes of the 1960s pitted younger urban dwellers against people from the country and the powerful Greek Orthodox Church. All of the changes led to frequent switches in government, as there was one prime minister after another. Usually, it was one of two men, Constantine Karamanlis (right) or George Papandreou (left).

By the mid-1960s, many Greeks expected the generals in the army to take over, but when the coup did happen, it was a group of three extreme right-wing colonels who had direct command of units in Athens and other important cities. They also had the support of a number of politicians and business leaders.

The "Colonel's Coup" turned into a military dictatorship that lasted from 1967 to 1974. A counter-coup by King Constantine II failed, and his exile ended the Greek monarchy, seemingly for good. During this time, virtually all civil rights were extinguished from Greece, the "clean" language of *Katharevousa* was again made the language of journalism and politics, and Greek history—meaning ancient Greek history—was the focus of history courses. (As a side note, *Katharevousa* has been made all but extinct today, as it has been replaced by *demotic* Greek—the "language of the people.") Anything deemed "anti-Greek" was attacked.

Under the colonels, some parts of the Greek economy thrived, mainly those who were already rich. Others stagnated. One problem that plagued Greece since before the time of Venizelos and was actually made worse by him was giving peasants their own land to work in exchange for political loyalty. In the long run, this harmed the Greek economy, for most agriculture remained small-scale, and Greece had remained dependent on food exports to varying degrees since before WWII. However, the idea of a pastoral Greece appealed to the colonels, particularly their chief, Colonel George Papadopoulos, who began the coup. He ran the dreaded secret police and ended up as the dictator of the entire country. He once publicly beat a journalist to a pulp for suggesting that a piece of ancient Greek art depicted male homosexuality, which the colonel insisted did not exist until communism developed. You get the idea.

The end of the colonels' dictatorship came in 1974 when they, like most dictators, overreached themselves. In the 1950s, 1960s, and early 1970s, the question of *enosis* with Greece came to the fore, this time from the large island of Cyprus, some five hundred miles from mainland Greece to the south of the Dodecanese Islands. For many centuries, Cyprus had a majority Greek population (77 percent in 1960, mostly in the capital of Nicosia and in the western part of the island) and a sizable minority Turkish population (mostly in the capital and in the east). In 1878, the island had been placed under British administration and protection, and it was annexed by the British in 1914.

After the war, Greek Cypriots would periodically call for a union with Greece, but this was resisted not only by Turkey (naturally) but also by the US and the UK, which did not want to see a war between its NATO partners or instability in the area. In the 1950s, violence between nationalist ethnic Greeks and Turks took place, often on the island. In 1960, after long negotiations in London and Switzerland, the island became an independent nation with a power-sharing agreement between the Greeks and Turks.

However, this was not enough for many of the more militant Greeks on the island, who were led by a charismatic and politically clever Greek Orthodox archbishop, Makarios. With the connivance of the colonels, Makarios urged the Greek nationalists to rise up, and the colonels sent arms and were preparing to send a contingent of troops when the Turks decided they had had enough.

On July 20th, 1973, the Turkish Army attacked Greek Cypriot positions, its jets bombed their positions, and the Turkish Navy cut the island off from the rest of the world. An international agreement was swiftly concluded to avoid a growing conflict, which Greece at this time would have easily lost, and to avoid further ethnic and combat bloodshed on the island. Today, Cyprus is a divided island, with an unrecognized semi-independent Turkish state in the north and the internationally recognized Republic of Cyprus in the south. The demilitarized zone between the two parts of the island stands as it did in 1973, and it is only populated by occasional United Nations patrols.

The Turkish "victory" in Cyprus spelled the end of the military regime in Greece. International pressure, the turning of former allies against the colonels, and huge anti-government demonstrations (some of which involved mass fatalities) caused the colonels' dictatorship to end. Papadopoulos was sentenced to death, as were many in his government. This was commuted to a life sentence, and he died in custody while in an Athens hospital in 1999.

Though the road has been rocky for Greece since the end of the dictatorship, thankfully, nothing like it has occurred since.

Conclusion

In the years since 1973, Greece has remained, at least in comparison with prior years, relatively stable and at peace. From the mid-1970s to the first decades of the 21st century, Greek politics remained as animated and contentious as ever, but it was violence-free. Governments and their policies have shifted to the left and the right, with the 1980s and much of the 1990s actually seeing a left-leaning government in power.

In the early 1990s, the nation of Yugoslavia broke apart and saw its various ethnic groups go to war with one another. The conflict was marked by much suffering and the return of genocide to the European continent for the first time since WWII. When the United States and NATO finally put an end to the war, an entirely new group of nations had come into existence. One of them was made up of people who called themselves "Macedonians." Right away, there were problems with Greece. By calling themselves Macedonians and their new nation Macedonia, which lay between Greece and Serbia on Greece's north-central border, many Greeks feared that at some time in the future, these "Macedonians" would make claims on the region of Greece that the Greeks themselves called Macedonia. Aside from the potential problems about the border, the Greeks believed the Slavic people were attempting to usurp the Greeks' claim on the legacy of Alexander the Great, an intense point of pride in Greece (intense may not actually describe it correctly).

Huge protests broke out in Greece, and some extreme nationalists even called for punitive military action against the new nation unless they changed their name. It appeared for a time that there was going to be an international crisis in the Balkans once again. Talks eventually established a new provisional name for the nation that was at least somewhat palatable to the Greeks: the Former Yugoslav Republic of Macedonia, widely known by its acronym of FYROM. In a way, this name established that the new country had existed north of Greece's present-day borders as a province of Yugoslavia. Though this settled the matter for a while, the people in FYROM were not happy with constantly being reminded that they had been part of a failed state, and many Greeks still had problems with the nomenclature. Finally, in 2019, Greek Prime Minister Alexis Tsipras and his counterpart in FYROM announced an agreement on a new name, North Macedonia, which seemed to satisfy most people in both nations.

While the arguments about the name of its newest neighbor were raging, the Great Recession of 2008-09 occurred. It hit Greece particularly hard. It was already running deficits and barely keeping up with repayments on loans from the European Economic Community (EEC), of which it is a member, the International Monetary Fund (IMF), and individual nations, specifically Germany and the United States. This was partially because of massive tax evasions from the bottom of the economic food chain to the top. Greece's economy went into a tailspin as a result. Greece was hit worse than almost any other nation in Europe. Massive layoffs of government workers, including police, which naturally means a large rise in crime, and unemployment in the rest of the country ensued. Unemployment reached over 30 percent at one point. Banks failed by the score. Protests against the successive governments took place virtually every day for years. Parties on both the extreme right and the extreme left gained members, and political violence occurred, thankfully not at previous levels.

For years, Greece had been essentially governed by the fathers, sons, and grandsons of existing political dynasties, but in the 2000s and into the 2010s, these families and their political parties seemed to be out of answers.

The entire situation was made worse by two things. First, the international community, led by Germany, demanded that Greece change the way it governed, collected taxes, and created budgets if it was to secure more loans to stay afloat. This was met with violent opposition by many groups, including a union of left-leaning political parties, one of which was known by its acronym **SYRIZA**, from its Greek name meaning "from the roots" and which came to power at various times throughout the first part of the 2000s. However, given the alternative, even **SYRIZA** eventually had to agree to a program of fiscal austerity in Greece, of which the government (as of this writing in 2021) is still feeling the effects.

The second major problem, which reached critical mass in 2015 and which was discussed in some detail at the beginning of this book, is the Middle East refugee problem. In 2015, the problem consisted of massive numbers pouring into Greece, hoping to make it to Germany and other parts of wealthier northern Europe. Today, the problem is the refugee camps in Greece, which came as a result of various countries closing their borders to the refugees, mostly those from Syria. As you read earlier, tensions along the border with Turkey over the refugee question are on the rise.

Let's end on a happy note, though. Greece, almost inexplicably, seemed to get a handle on what to do about the COVID-19 pandemic of 2020-21. Comparatively speaking, Greece had a lesser rate of both infection and death than almost any other developed country. Part of that was the close feeling of community that still exists in much of Greece. Take a look at the article on the island of Chios in the bibliography for details on how this happened. As of this writing,

Greece has opened its borders to tourists of most countries, including the United States. Perhaps time will tell, but for now, things seem to be looking up.

Here's another book by Captivating History that you might like

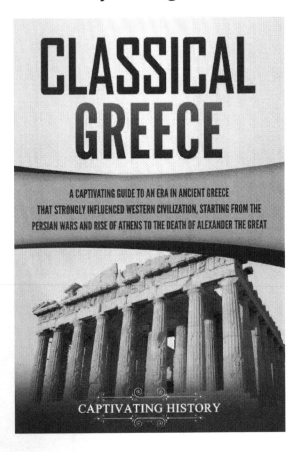

Free Bonus from Captivating History (Available for a Limited time)

Hi History Lovers!

Now you have a chance to join our exclusive history list so you can get your first history ebook for free as well as discounts and a potential to get more history books for free! Simply visit the link below to join.

Captivatinghistory.com/ebook

Also, make sure to follow us on Facebook, Twitter and Youtube by searching for Captivating History.

Bibliography

Beaton, Roderick. GREECE: BIOGRAPHY OF A MODERN NATION. Chicago: University	of Chicago Press, 2021.

Beevor, Antony. CRETE: THE BATTLE AND THE RESISTANCE. London: John Murray, 2011.

Brewer, David. THE GREEK WAR OF INDEPENDENCE: THE STRUGGLE FOR FREEDOM AND THE BIRTH OF MODERN GREECE. New York: Abrams, 2011.

"Chios Massacre: The Worst Atrocity Committed by the Ottomans Against Greeks." GreekReporter.com. Last modified February 6, 2021. https://greekreporter.com/2020/03/29/chios-massacre-the-worst-atrocity-committed-by-the-ottomans-against-greeks/

"Controversial New Labour Laws Set to Shake Up Working Life in Greece." The Guardian. Last modified June 17, 2021. https://www.theguardian.com/world/2021/jun/17/greece-controversial-new-labour-law-reform-shake-up-working-life

Contoudis, John. CHIOS: A HISTORY. River Vale, NJ: Cosmos Publishing, 2009.

Durant, Will. THE LIFE OF GREECE: THE STORY OF CIVILIZATION. New York: Simon & Schuster, 2011.

"Exploring Greece's Unseen Corners." The New York Times - Breaking News, US News, World News and Videos. Last modified June 15, 2021. https://www.nytimes.com/2021/06/14/travel/greece-traditions.html?smid=em-share.

Gage, Nicholas. ELENI. New York: Ballantine Books, 2010.

"The Greco-Italian War: One of Benito Mussolini's Biggest Failures."
Warfare History Network. Last modified September 25, 2020.
https://warfarehistorynetwork.com/2017/07/20/the-greco-italian-war-one-of-
benito-mussolinis-biggest-failures/

"Greco-Turkish War, 1919-22." HistoryNet.
https://www.historynet.com/greco-turkish-war-1919-22.htm

"Greek Nationalism, the 'Megale Idea' and Venizelism to 1923."
Redirecting. Accessed July 12, 2021.
https://staff.lib.msu.edu/sowards/balkan/lect14.htm

"HOW A SLAVE GIRL BECAME AN OTTOMAN QUEEN." (2019, January 17). OZY.
https://www.ozy.com/true-and-stories/how-a-slave-girl-became-an-ottoman-
queen/88876/

"Katharevousa Vs. Demotiki: The Unknown History of Modern Greek."
Nicholas C. Rossis. Last modified December 6, 2019.
https://nicholasrossis.me/2014/11/21/katharevousa-vs-demotiki-the-
unknown-history-of-modern-greek/

"List of Massacres During the Greco-Turkish War (1919–22)." Wikipedia
– Encyclopedia.
https://au.vvikipedla.com/wiki/List_of_massacres_during_the_Greco-
Turkish_War_(1919%E2%80%9322)

"Macedonia and Greece: Vote Settles 27-year Name Dispute." BBC News.
Last modified January 25, 2019. https://www.bbc.com/news/world-europe-
47002865

Mazower, M. (2007). SALONICA, CITY OF GHOSTS: CHRISTIANS, MUSLIMS AND
JEWS   1430-1950. Vintage

The New Arab & agencies. (March 2020). *"TURKEY FIRES TEAR GAS AT GREEK
BORDER GUARDS AS REFUGEE STANDOFF CONTINUES."* The New Arab.
https://english.alaraby.co.uk/news/turkey-fires-tear-gas-greek-border-guards

"On This Island, Everyone Knows Your Name (if You Have Covid-19)."
The New York Times - Breaking News, US News, World News and
Videos. Last modified September 18, 2020.
https://www.nytimes.com/2020/09/17/world/europe/greece-chios-
coronavirus.html

Psaropoulos, John. "How Poetry Won Independence for Greece." WSJ.
Last modified April 8, 2021. https://www.wsj.com/articles/how-poetry-won-
independence-for-greece-11617906113?mod=flipboard

Ureneck, Lou. SMYRNA, SEPTEMBER 1922: ONE AMERICAN'S MISSION TO RESCUE VICTIMS OF THE 20TH CENTURY'S FIRST GENOCIDE. New York: HarperCollins, 2015.

"WAS COLUMBUS GREEK?" (n.d.). Matt Barrett's Guides to Greece and the Greek Islands. https://www.greecetravel.com/history/columbus/

Printed in Great Britain
by Amazon